For Life We Learn

Portrait taken approx. 1972/73

For Life We Learn

The Life Story of Geoff Blackmore
December 1936 to October 2021

Geoff Blackmore

For Life We Learn
Geoff Blackmore

Published by Aspect Design, 2022

Designed, printed and bound by Aspect Design
89 Newtown Road, Malvern, Worcs. WR14 1PD
United Kingdom
Tel: 01684 561567
E-mail: allan@aspect-design.net
Website: www.aspect-design.net

A copy of this book has been deposited
with the British Library Board

Original cover image of Mount Hermon School,
Darjeeling by Geoff Blackmore.

ISBN 9781912078479

Contents

Chapter One
My Early Years

My parents, Hubert Henry Blackmore and Winifred Jessie Harse were married at Moorland Road Congregational Church, Weston-super-Mare, Somerset on 16 October 1926.

He was twenty-four and she nearly a year younger. Father was a journeyman baker, and mother was a book-keeper in a butcher's business. So, bread and meat came together!

The Blackmore family had moved to Weston from the Bridgwater area. They had nine children – five sons and four daughters. My father was the middle one of the nine. By the time I was born three of the daughters had died. Alice, who survived, became my godmother.

The Harse family were Weston people. Mother's father was a painter and decorator until failing sight restricted his activities. He died before my birth. The children's work would have been vital for the family of four. There was one boy and three girls. My mother was the eldest. They lived in a substantial stone house in Totterdown Road

My parents' wedding

My father delivering bread by motorcycle

alongside the railway loop from Weston station towards Bridgwater and Taunton. The house was named Claremont and was probably built by the builders of Claremont Crescent overlooking the seafront in northern Weston. My great grandparents lived there. His name was Chalmers and was a well-known stone-mason. One of the family was employed in the building of the beautiful spire of St Mary Redcliffe in Bristol, completed in 1872.

My parents were to spend the first eight years of their married life on the move – always in rented, related or tied accommodation. It could have been rooms over a bakery shop, or the house of relatives recently returned from Rhodesia, needing home care. Mother was an excellent housekeeper and longed for a home of her own. My brother, John Chalmers, was born in November 1928, and the problems he had as a baby may have been linked with the rheumatic fever that mother developed. She was very ill with this life-threatening disease, but in 1933 the future looked bright enough for a deposit to be paid for a newly-built house on Bedminster Down, Bristol. They moved in during 1934, named it Westway because it caught the setting sun over the hill, casting a shadow over the house front. It was on the end of a terrace with ample garden space on three sides. Mother was a green-fingered gardener, and with improving health she was in her element. By mid-1936 she knew that her second child was on the way.

The author as a child

Father's vital work as a baker had seen them through the Depression Years, He worked long hours delivering the bread baked by E. Luton & Sons in their bakery in Bedminster, Bristol. With thirteen and half hours of 1936 still to pass, their second son was safely delivered in a Bristol Maternity Hospital.

That was the first mistake I made. I was a boy! It caused me to have three names. Mother had wanted a girl, to name her Margaret after a dear friend, Margaret Owen. So, she decided to call me Owen. Her sister, Nell, contacted her to point out that my initials would be GOB, not a name to go to school with! She suggested I be called David, too. So here I am, Geoffrey, David, Owen Blackmore ever since!

BEDMINSTER DOWN

Let's look more closely at the house to which Baby Geoffrey was brought early in 1937. When numbers were later applied it became

66 Eastlyn Road

number 66. The house next, a different style, was 62. I often wondered what had happened to 64! The road was named Eastlyn, and was macadamized up to our house. Then it remained stony until well after the Second World War.

The house looked larger being on the end of the terrace. It had a bay window at the front and all transom windows and the front door had coloured glass. Within the bay was the front room, a special room only used on Sundays, when a fire might be lit. Against one wall was a highly polished upright piano. My later practice times could be cold half hours! The furniture was hard and square-with corded edges. The fabric was rather rough to a child's hand

The new baby, however, would be taken to the back room –the 'living room'. This was a much warmer and lighter room, with highly polished lino on the floor. A dining table with four high backed chairs, a settee and two arm chairs, rounded and upholstered – all much more comfortable than the front room. (This was to be my home for the next twenty-four years!) The room centred upon the fireplace-regularly blackened and polished. From two side hobs, a kettle could be moved over the flames. The fire was lit for much of the year – certainly, on that cold January day when my Mother brought me home. She immediately looked for the remains of the Christmas cake she had made, but only crumbs remained after being attacked by a husband, the lodger and eight-year-old John.

I mention lodgers. Over the years, a number of individuals and couples were to occupy the two larger rooms at the front of the house. It was a way of helping friends from Weston looking for work in Bristol. It, too, must have been a means of paying off the mortgage on the new house. It took many years to pay off the £500 needed. The lodger in 1937 was Ken Gundry. He was of a Weston family and was learning his skills in the upholstery and carpeting business. He was a talented musician, a keen angler, and a great talker. We always

Ken Gundry with Mother and myself

knew him as 'Uncle'. He and his wife, Doris, were later to be good, kind friends, especially when setting up our first home. A couple to be married from our home were Albert and Rose Parker. He was a soldier, away from home for long periods. Their eldest son, Robert, was another new baby to be brought though the front door.

Later there was Allan Barnes, a bank clerk at Barclays in Weston, about to be transferred to Bedminster, Bristol. He remained a friend of the family for many years, and is an example of people who have enriched my life through its course. He asked me to be his best man when he married a young lady he had met at our church, thus acknowledging his love for my mother and her family.

Where was that baby to sleep back in 1937? There were three bedrooms and an upstairs bathroom and toilet, (not all the houses had such luxury), but mother always wanted the best for her family.

'Uncle Ken' had the large front bedroom, John would be in the small room, so Baby Geoffrey would start his sleeping days in a cot beside his parents' double bed in the back room. There was a small, tiled fireplace, where a fire was only lit when someone was ill. Above it was Mother's favourite picture – in black and white – Holman Hunt's *The Light of the World*.

The bathroom boasted a shining, copper gas geyser. Lighting this would cause a frightening 'plop,' but it meant we had instant hot water upstairs. The small bedroom for many years was to be mine, and this was a cold room with two 'outside' walls. There was only room for a single bed, a small dressing table and a corner 'hanging wardrobe'. Shelves above the bed held my books.

Beyond the back door steep steps led down to a large garden – the pride and joy of my parents. Whatever mother put in seemed to grow. There were tomatoes, raspberries, black currents, rows of vegetables, and flowers beneath a plum tree that never produced any fruit. Rhubarb grew on the slopes of the Anderson Air-raid shelter with huge gooseberries around it.

WORLD WAR

This brings me to my earliest memory that of being carried from my warm cot, out into the cold garden air on my way to the shelter, where a bunk bed awaited. Sometimes neighbours joined us if their menfolk were away. Having read of all that went on in Bristol during the six years of the war, I realize how much my parents shielded me from the impact made on families and their homes at that time. They tried to make life as 'normal' as possible –perhaps especially for John who was old enough to remember pre-war days.

Bristol was badly 'blitzed,' and I was to grow up fully aware of the damage done. Much of it was caused by fire, and the sky glowed red towards the city as we emerged from the shelter when the 'All Clear' sounded. Next day, if we ventured down the hill, we might see the shell of huge buildings and perhaps watch as toppling walls were pulled to the ground. Housing in Bedminster was devastated, but up on the 'Down' only occasional damage was caused by the off-loading of bombs by departing aircraft. My brother, John, was 'evacuated' to Weston when the Bristol Blitz was driving hundreds of people

Anderson Air Raid Shelter

into the countryside every night. No sooner was he established at Aunt Alice's house in Moorland Road than the bombers turned their attention to Weston. The lower end of that road was badly hit; a Laundry was gutted; the little church on the corner was blown sideways, and bridges over the railway were twisted. I remember actually crossing the lines to reach the bombed home of Mother's brother, Jack, and his family. They were lucky to survive.

Visits to Weston both during the war and after were always special events. We walked down to Parson Street Station-surrounded by bomb sites – and caught the steam train for the twenty-mile trip to Weston. Excitement was particularly high at Christmas with presents under a tree in Grandma's big Front Room. We children were not allowed in before the appointed time for opening the door. The presents, if toys, were usually 'hand-downs'. New toys were scarce during the war. Lighting in that part of the house was by gas. The big bedroom where we slept could only be reached by candle light, and I remember the feather mattress that awaited us – delightfully soft and warm.

Chapter Two
School Years

SCHOOL BEGINS

I started school at Bedminster Down Junior Mixed School in September 1941. I was in the Infants' Department for two years before transferring across the big playground to the Junior Section. A big change came to our lives, when in November 1942 Father was called up to serve in the Army as a driver. This was in preparation for the D Day landings in June 1944. He drove in convoys of military vehicles, gathered in London, and then driven down to the South coast in readiness for the Invasion of Normandy. It must have been so different from driving a baker's

van! He, himself, was never to cross the channel. He had a fall from a vehicle and badly damaged his left leg. He was invalided out in January 1945. He was to suffer pain in that leg for many years after.

I was proud of my 'soldier Dad' and remember my picture of him was pinned to the Class 7 wall. His many pockets were much in evidence. I recall the sadness of waving goodbye to

Dad in Army Uniform

him as his train left Temple Meads Station after a weekend leave in September 1943.

These were years of development as I progressed through the Junior School. My route was by way of classes 5, 3, and finally 1. My memories of early teachers are vague, often concerned with punishment. One wore black ribbon in her hair – we were convinced that she was a German spy, especially, as she lifted short, trouser legs to slap fleshy thighs! One male teacher seemed determined to 'ruler' every child. I received mine for not closing my book quickly enough.

My Junior School

Books were becoming more important in my life. Grandma introduced me to the Rupert stories –cutting and sticking the daily episodes from the 'Daily Express'.

When she cut the story part off by mistake, she would invent her own story to

Grandma Harse

go with it. So, I began to write my own stories, too. Books became favourite presents for me. I liked historical stories, and then those describing life in distant lands. There was a series of *Twin* stories – *Swiss Twins, Eskimo Twins, Chinese Twins* – all pre-war dated, of course. In the school store room, next to the Hall, I saw a large relief model of South America, with the mountains upstanding and fascinating to the touch of fingers destined to teach geography!

VE Day (8 May 1945) was a time no one living would forget! There was a street party, bonfires and dancing round the streets. I particularly remember walking with Mum to St Mary Redcliffe Church in Bristol and hearing, for the first time, church bells pealing.

Rupert cutting from *Daily Express*

Revd Steve and wife Betty in
Scout Uniform

We were so thankful that the war was
over. It was a time for spiritual renewal
for Mum. She was confirmed into
the Anglican Church – you couldn't
receive Holy Communion unless you
were. During the war years she was
much involved in a welfare clinic held
in the Parish Hall. She had charge of
supplementary items like cod liver oil
capsules, concentrated orange juice
and malt extract – delicious on bread
and butter!

THE ANGLICAN CHURCH

All this drew Mum into the
fellowship at St Oswald's Church
on Bedminster Down. A vacancy in
the ministry there was filled in 1946
by a young vicar, fresh from the team
that had done such wonderful work
at St Martin in the Fields in Central
London throughout the war. That
church was already famous for its
music and singing, so the Revd Steve
Osborne and Betty, his wife, were to
uplift the singing at St Oswalds in a
remarkable way

Into this I was drawn. I was already
singing in the school choir which
combined with other schools to
sing in big concerts in the city. This

encouraged me to join the church choir being revitalised by Steve Osborne. He activated a revolutionary idea of moving the choir stalls from the chancel to the rear of the congregation and near to the organ. So, all the singing was vastly improved. There were some very good voices in that choir, especially among the young ladies.

Revd Steve Osborne leads St Oswalds' Choir

Class 1 at primary school (me in front row, second from right)

Solos were encouraged. My first was a verse from 'It Came Upon the Midnight Clear' at a carol service by candlelight. A bigger challenge was 'Hear my Prayer', which leads to 'O For the Wings of a Dove', which the other leading choirboy sang. During sermons, I found myself squinting at candle flames, which did nothing to improve my young eyesight. By the time I was in the top class I was wearing glasses, and have done so ever since. My teacher, Mrs Richards, was excellent, with standards very high indeed. The Honour Boards of the school reflect this in the large number of grammar school entries from her classes.

TEENAGE YEARS

After the Butler Act of 1944, eleven-year-old children took an examination to decide where their secondary education would be. Bristol had a number of grammar schools, some of ancient foundation. Queen Elizabeth Hospital (QEH) was one of these, founded in 1586 to educate orphan boys. They were to wear the

Admiring my brother (eight years older) in Scout Uniform

Bluecoats as did the boys of Christ's Hospital in London. I sat the Entrance Examination of this school, but was unsuccessful. Then in early 1947, when I sat the 11+ exam, I did sufficiently well to be granted a City Junior Scholarship and a place as a day scholar at QEH! (Two other boys from Mrs Richards' class passed the entrance exam and were to board there.)

A word about Scouting – (a movement then not forty years

old). John was a Scout as soon as he was old enough. There is a photo of myself looking enviously at him in his uniform – stiff brimmed hat and all! His troop was associated with the local Zion Methodist Church. During the war the leaders were called up, but as soon as it was finished, John was back. He was a sincere Scout, and (later) a leader until his dying day, still a member of that chapel troop. When at the age of enrolment, I was encouraged to join the new troop being set up at the Church. I was reluctant, but for some reason, never clear to me, John did not want me to join his troop. So, somewhat reluctantly, I turned to the new one at St Oswald's. John, later, accepted me, after my fifteenth birthday, as a senior Scout, then as a Rover Scout.

With my deteriorating eye sight seemed to go a problem of speaking. A stammer developed which to some degree has never left me. As a junior child it was particularly bad and it made life very difficult for me. The one thing that gave me hope was that I never stammered when I was singing. It seemed to stem from poor breathing, particularly when I was lacking in confidence and in nervous situations. Words beginning with vowels and certain letters like *br* and *pr* would often cause a stammer. I can't remember when it started, but it has been a long challenging process to achieve the career and calling to which I felt drawn. When, later, I was training students for elocution events, I often had a secret smile to myself!

HOLIDAYS

I pause for a word about family holidays. In 1945 we travelled by train to Paignton, South Devon. This apparently had been a holiday destination before the war. We were clearly known by the ladies running the guest house, as they took our ration books on arrival! A happening there illustrates my growing money-sense. I had saved for a long time for a new cricket bat. Eventually, we went

Playing cricket with Dad with my new bat

to a sports shop in Bristol and bought a splendid blade. I only had enough money left to buy a cheap 'composition' cricket ball. Both I took to Paignton. There was a grassy playground near our lodgings and Dad and I went there to play. It might have been the hardness of the ball, or the way the bat hit the ground, but to my dismay, a chunk of the blade flew off! I was devastated! 'All that saving'! A roll of white sticky tape was bought and the chunk fastened into place, but it never seemed the same again. I have always been careful with money and to look for quality and value in what I buy. I think it all began with that bat!

Dad's new car KHW 3 with myself and Kenneth Price

In 1947 Father bought his new car, an Austin 8 (£475).

That was another long save! John and I were asked to contribute to the cost of its number plates – £1 from John and 5/ – from me. (That was probably Mum's idea!) With great care that car was waxed and polished, especially before a long trip on holiday. Having the car, gave us so much more flexibility. We were in Bournemouth when we learned of my new school. We had relatives there, like Great Aunt Ida, and she was a single lady of great size and love.

Queen Elizabeth's Hospital, Bristol>

QUEEN ELIZABETH'S HOSPITAL

By September I was ready for my new school – equipped with a new uniform, cap and sports kit. We gathered, parents and boys, in the School Hall. 'Please stand when the Headmaster enters,' we were instructed. And in he swept, cap and gowned! In slow languid tones, Mr Gillett bade us welcome. Parents had to declare that their sons would remain at the school until they were sixteen and had obtained their School Certificates. 'We expect them all to do so!' he added. The lowest Form, (not class) was Form 11, having about thirty-five boys – 'the best boys from many schools in Bristol,' Mother was told later. Much of the work was new to me. I had never learned Latin or French, or tackled woodwork. Clearly, I was not going to be a star pupil. New, too, was the long journey to school-instead of the ten-minute walk twice a day for so long. There were lessons on a Saturday morning, too. I soon discovered

Myself in the QEH uniform of a day scholar (1947)

that as a City Scholarship boy I was entitled to a daily bus pass, clipped for each journey by the conductor. There was a bus from Bedminster Down to the top of Park Street – then a quick run to the school gates. A missed bus could mean lateness and trouble! Later, I was able to cycle to school – and was given a grant towards its maintenance! But still I was often late, held up by closing bridges at the Docks, or taking longer over my newspaper round. Lateness continued to be a failing throughout my school career.

School days were not happy days. I was small in stature, bespectacled and liable to stammer. I became a centre for bullying by larger boys, usually boarders. They loved to pick on my connections with Scouting. When translating our Latin books, I would sit in terror as I spotted references to 'explorates' in the passage ahead. I wished that Caesar didn't keep sending out scouts ahead of his armies!

In a school taking pride in sport, I was too little to have much impact in games like rugby. These were compulsory and involved a long journey to the playing fields on the northern edge of Bristol. This is why cycling became my form of transport. The cycle ride home took at least an hour from one side of the city to the other. One day I was particularly late after being found at the base of a scrummage, (I was always hooker, being small) with a broken collar bone. A member of staff had taken me to the Infirmary for treatment and then brought me home in his car. That collar-bone mend still shows up on X rays! Miscounting the balls in a cricket over, I received the sixth ball in my teeth resulting in a gap ever since.

Academically, I progressed slowly through a lower stream of talent, Forms II; IIIb; III; IV; and V. Even then my age meant I was too young to take GCE. You had to be sixteen in September. I didn't reach that age until New Year's Eve. This meant a continuation into the Sixth form in order to take three essential O-level subjects, for entry into university. By this time I was enjoying the smaller tutorial groups in the Sixth, specialising on chosen subjects. Studying for O-levels held me back somewhat. Latin was never easy; physics required maths, which I had never understood, and English language, which was fine. I passed in all three, so could then concentrate on my geography, history and English literature. It took me another two years in the Sixth form to gain Advanced Levels in geography and history, and another O-level in literature. My success in geography owes much to my teacher, Donald Thatcher. I took note of his methods and many of his diagrams and simple pictures were to be used later in my own teaching of the subject. My examination success was enough to win me a Bristol Senior Scholarship to study for a general honours degree at Bristol University, but the start of that was to be delayed for two memorable years.

First, I would like to mention some school friends. My friendship with Roger Billings lasted through all my eight years at QEH. It flourished not in

My friends Roger Billings and Robert Rowland with repaired cricket bat!

The Pirates of Penzance (QEH operatta). Author is third from right.

'Jesus turned and looked at Peter'

school, for we were in different forms, but in our homes. Our parents became good friends and we shared several holidays. Often Roger and I played Book Cricket at home, and sometimes the real game, with another friend, Robert Rowland. I used to cycle to school with Robert, and on our homeward journeys we often cycled round the docks to 'collect' the names and cargoes of ships from distant ports and countries. Robert's father managed a cinema in East Bristol and his influence enabled Robert (and his friends!) to enter freely into many places of entertainment in the city. His mother was well known at the BBC in Bristol, and Robert was later to find a career with them.

I must mention, too, that QEH introduced me to the Gilbert and Sullivan operettas. Whilst still a treble, I took part in the school presentations of *Trial by Jury* and then as one of General Stanley's daughters in the *Pirates of Penzance*. The thrill of being back stage, and then on the stage, was to stay with me for many years to come.

During my school days, I became more spiritually affected through the ministry at St Oswald's Church. Revd Steve Osborne was there from 1946–54. Several of the Sunday School teachers also influenced me through those formative years. Steve was a good story – teller, as I remember when, through one Holy Week, he enthralled us with what happened to Jesus through those days. His Confirmation classes thoughtfully prepared us for that important step in our lives. In one corner of his study was a large picture of Jesus entitled 'The Lord turned and looked at Peter' (that is when the cock crowed). Wherever you sat in that room, Jesus appeared to be looking straight at you. It was a picture that followed me through my National Service, appearing in each camp church! Before confirmation on 21 October 1951, the baptism of an adult was held, and Steve, then, turned and shook my hand in welcome, explaining that I had been christened in a Congregational Church!

In 1952 Steve wrote a pageant

Revd Steve Osborne with church wardens

to commemorate the twenty-fifth anniversary of the building of the church in 1927. It told the story of Oswald, King of Northumbria, who died in 642 of battle wounds inflicted by the pagan Mercians. I remember a procession around the church with Oswald at its head, his sword inverted to make a cross held high. We sang 'Take My Life and Let It Be Consecrated Lord to Thee.' It was a moment of personal commitment.

Memorable, too, was the first of Steve's Good Friday Processions that were made all around the parish on Bedminster Down. A plain wooden cross was made, and carried by a succession of people along the roads. Steve, in a black cope, walked behind it, followed by the choir, also in black. It poured with rain! We were drenched! I remember seeing Steve turning around at one point, rain streaming down his face – but lit up with joy, when he saw the long line of parishioners walking behind. I lost count of the number of times we stopped to sing 'When I survey the wondrous cross' with Steve's voice ringing out, as he explained what we were doing and why. A prayer would be said for those living nearby. I have never forgotten that day. Was that when a calling to ministry stirred within me? It might well have been.

I was encouraged to take an interest in the work of the Church Overseas. One of my boyhood heroes had been David Livingstone, and, on telling Mum that I, too, would like to be a 'mystery' to Africa, she replied that I was sure to be that, if I ever got there!

Mother, herself, was, as a member of the PCC, a worker on the Overseas Committee of the Church. She was responsible for the collecting, opening and re-distributing the Missionary boxes. I enjoyed helping her – particularly in counting the money! The church held two Missionary Weekends each year, supporting SPG and CMS, equally. I learned more about the work in Africa, and was able to update much of my school geography with pamphlets gleaned from the Societies. As our school text books were mostly pre-war publications, this was very useful. As a calling to ministry strengthened, it turned, increasingly, towards working overseas. This naturally seemed to involve ordination, and I became known as an 'ordinand.' I was elected to the PCC, and becoming the chairman of the Overseas Committee, I tried to interest people more in interdenominational missions. The Mission to Lepers, as it was known, particularly interested me.

But how could this basically shy lad with a pronounced stammer contemplate such a calling and career? Several developments helped. St Oswald's Youth Fellowship began to play mixed-hockey! This was a game I could actually play wearing my spectacles-although not as goalkeeper! There were a number of mixed clubs in Bristol. Our 'home' pitch was far away on Durdham Downs – with no changing rooms or nets for the goals. We had league and cup matches. I became fixture secretary for the club, and this involved me in contacting other clubs, and our own players when games were cancelled. We had no telephone at home, so I had to resort to using a call box some 100 yards away. Telephone! I had never used it without stammering. But this I had to overcome. It was not easy, but by licking my lips and breathing deeply and slowly, my speech gradually improved!

Another help came from Mother. For years, I had suffered the torment of piano lessons with an elderly lady (so she seemed) living in a tall, gloomy house in Bedminster. I lied my way out of as many encounters with her as possible. When my deceit was discovered, mother labelled every item in my bedroom with reference to the 'liar' who used it. It was a lesson I never forgot. Anyway, she sought the help of my headmaster, (no less!) to ask him to find a teacher of elocution to help me with my speech. The piano lessons had to end, as she could not afford both. Learning to recite poems may have sharpened my memory but did little to assist me in normal conversation. However, I was to find the ability to play simple tunes on a piano, and to read music for singing, very useful later in life.

It was my intention to offer for ministry that led me to opt for National Service in 1955. I was well past my eighteenth birthday, overdue for call-up. Many of my friends at school with university places secured, opted out of National Service. By the time they qualified, National Service had finished, and they were able to continue their careers. Roger Billings was such a one. As an ordinand, I was advised to do my military training as it would be a good experience for anyone intending to enter the ministry. Only time would tell!

I was due to start my training in September. In July I spent time working in Luton's Bakery with my dad. I enjoyed night work slicing bread, and then going with him on his morning round in a van full of newly-baked loaves. The smell of fresh bread still reminds me of those days. He served shops, hospitals and Mental Homes in Bath, Bradford on Avon, and Melksham. He was offered cups of tea in most places – he seldom refused! All this was useful work experience and personal contact.

Chapter Three
RAF Leads to Romance

ROYAL AIR FORCE

Reporting for duty in the Royal Air Force on 7 September 1955 was the biggest step in my life since starting at QEH. This time I was on my own! The journeys from Bristol to London and to Bedford were my longest undertaken on my own. I had to report to RAF Cardington-still dominated by the huge hanger of the ill-fated R101 airship. It took just a week to kit us out, test us, medically exam

RAF Boys at Camp

us and send us on our way to a basic training camp. It was decided that I was 'officer material', so I found myself at RAF Hednesford on Cannock Chase in Staffordshire.

This meant that my companions had all been well educated, having either been to university, or were intending to go. Each billet had a 'Senior Man' and ours was a graduate by the name of George Bennett. He was a Christian, four years older than most of us. He had completed his training for teaching, so was ready to start his career on leaving the air force. He was to have a considerable influence on my life.

The next eight weeks were spent on 'Square bashing'. The corporals in charge of this were from the RAF Regiment (soldier/airmen) whose main task was to defend airfields and other installations. They were extremely smart and efficient. They not only trained us in drill but also in rifle handling and shooting. One corporal occupied a small room in each billet. Ours was called Gus, and I remember him asking us to buy him some curtain material on a visit to Lichfield. He was a nice chap; better spoken than most of his comrades. One weekend of our training involved us in marching across the Chase to an R&I Camp where we spent two nights under canvas; and did pioneering projects similar to those I had done in John's Rover Crew. It was good to be out in the crisp, autumn air.

I had met another ordinand at an SPG Summer School back in August. He lived in Birmingham and had invited me to attend his church if ever I was near that city. I found it was a short rail journey through 'darkest Walsall' on Sunday mornings. Rising early, I had a Day Return to meet with this friend in Handsworth. After church, I was invited to Sunday Lunch at the home of a Mr and Mrs Hunt. What a meal I had! What a sleep before a roaring fire! What a tea before heading to catch an evening train. On two further Sundays, I did the same again! Wonderful to meet Christians in action!

After five weeks came the longed for '48' – the first chance to go home for a weekend. Buses set off in all directions. One took me to Bristol. How good it was to be at home! One of the new things I spotted there was a television set. Mum and Dad had decided that, now my school studies were passed, they could have a set.

At home on the First '48' weekend

I returned to Hednesford on the Sunday evening with some trepidation. On Monday we were due to have our 'jabs'. I remember one of our hulking lads (he rowed at school) fainted from the affect of these injections. I played an arm-swinging game of hockey in the afternoon and was unaffected by them. The next three weeks passed with final tests in various aspects of our training, especially one that tested our suitability for different trades in the RAF. I was pleased that both George and I were included in the batch to begin Trade Training in Signals at Compton Bassett in Wiltshire.

George was now much farther from his home in Yorkshire, so I invited him to come at week ends with me to Bristol. We went to the Theatre Royal on his birthday in January. The course lasted thirteen weeks and I went home most weekends. First thing on a Monday morning I bought a ticket to Bristol for the next weekend!

We spent the first two weeks of the course learning to type. All day, for ten days, we pounded the covered keyboards. We had to reach an accurate speed of about twenty-five words a minute. This, for me, was by far the most useful skill learned in the RAF.

When I think of all the exam papers and play scripts I was to type in the future, I am still grateful for that training. We were to be 'tape relay operators' in a Signal Station. So, we had to be able to read long paper strips whose pattern of holes spelt out a message. As it was winter, I phoned the Officer i/c Hockey, and told him I had played for a prominent team in Bristol (we were bottom of the league!). He invited me to play for the Station team and so I enjoyed several Wednesday afternoons trips to play other station teams – both RAF and Army. The course came to an end and we lined up to learn our postings. They could have been overseas as the RAF signals network is world-wide. However, I was to go to the Hub of the network at the Central Signal Station at RAF Stanbridge in Bedfordshire. I was delighted that George was also to go there.

SIGNALS SENT AND RECEIVED

We were billeted at RAF Bletchley in Buckinghamshire. We were to work shifts, so there was a daily ten-mile journey in little

Message tapes from a Priority Bag – with Valentine card

RAF gharries – with slatted wooden seats – to take us down to Leighton Buzzard (a pleasant market town near the Grand Union Canal) and then another two miles on to Stanbridge.

The shifts were Middles (midnight to 8 am), Days 8 am–5 pm, and Evenings 5 pm to midnight. We took most of our meals at Stanbridge. The time within the Station was always GMT. Much of our time we worked in a large hall lined with

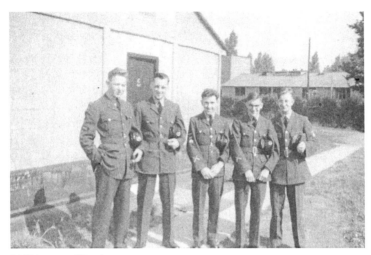

SASRA group of friends

tape relay machines and teleprinters. These were linked by radio and landlines with RAF Signal stations around the UK and in many distant lands. The busiest line was to the Air Ministry in London. Stations in Germany were busy, too, as was that to Cyprus, especially during the Suez Crisis. Ceylon had further connections throughout the Far East. Ottawa was our American station. Messages were graded as to the length of time for handling them –from Deferred (could take two days), Routine (one day), to Operational Immediate (fifteen minutes), to Flash (instant handling). Each message of holed tapes was put in an appropriate coloured bag to be tossed onto a conveyor belt for further directing. It had to be me who put a Flash in a Routine bag! We had been snow-balling before going on duty and my specs were damaged. I was not seeing too well. I was directed to clear a pile of tape spewing from a machine. I did this as quickly as I could. Most of the messages were routine, but there was just one zz Flash in the middle of them which I failed to spot. When the mistake was discovered I had to explain my handicap. It was not too serious as the message was to cancel an earlier zz which had warned certain aircrews to stand by on alert. Because of my mistake they continued on stand by for longer than was necessary. That it could have been more serious was impressed upon me. My mates never let me forget, either!

My spiritual growth and development was enriched when I discovered SASRA, an interdenominational group that introduce Readers into military establishments. There were just two members at Bletchley – a WAAF catering sergeant and an airman in accounts. They were praying for more, when George and I walked in! We had managed to get ourselves into a billet of Christian lads – dominated by Salvationists. So we had fine fellowship during our off-duty hours. We met as a group and went out as a group. So, when George heard from a young lady he and his fiancée had met on a Methodist Holiday, that she was attending a week of meetings at a college in London, it was decided that the whole SASRA group would join her there on Thursday 5 July 1956.

In civies with SASRA badge

JUDITH MAY PRINCE

We met Judith Prince – a trainee nurse – at Euston Station. George introduced her to us. I could not shake hands, as I was holding a cup of tea! We went by underground to Southgate. The last part of the journey was in daylight. I could see large houses and big green parks, giving me a new, pleasing impression of London. So much was new to me that day! I was experiencing,

increasingly, the fellowship of
Christians from other denominations,
particularly Salvationists, Methodists
and Baptists. The preaching and
singing at the North London Keswick
Convention meeting was inspiring. I
was determined to learn more.

So, two nights later, found me
there again – this time on my own!
It was the final meeting of the week
–and it finished on a high. I hoped
Judith was somewhere in the crowded
marquee. I slipped out during the
final hymn and stood in the gateway.
She had a hairstyle that was short at
the back (like a thatch cottage) and
I was afraid I would only recognise

Judith Prince on an early date (1956)

her from behind! I saw her; I called out – nervously – she stopped,
and smiled in recognition. We walked together down to Southgate
Station – into a future that we have now shared for sixty five years!

That summer of 1956 was to be a time of change in my life,
spiritually, emotionally and physically. My contacts with other
Christians were to continue alongside an increasing attraction to
Judy, as she liked to be called. We met again at an International
Salvationist Rally at the Royal Albert Hall. The music, the singing,
the brass band playing, threatened to raise the roof! We finished the
evening broadcasting for 'Sunday Half-Hour'. Judy was there with
another nurse, and it was the first time we had stood together in an
act of worship. Soon after, I had a week's leave to attend another
SPG Summer School at Bournemouth. This was memorable on
account of it being the first time I had encountered opposition

to my connexions with other denominations. I was still an SPG ordinand, so the Supervisor was much concerned. He was a High Anglican and had no room for Salvationists who don't 'believe in Holy Communion!' I was very disturbed by all this, and didn't know which way to turn (career to follow). I had little contact with my home church at that time. I was enjoying my times with my new friends. My girl-friend was a Methodist who was soon to start training for her SRN qualification, with missionary work in mind.

LETTERS LEAD TO LOVE

A very important feature of our relationship during the initial months was letter-writing. I found this to be an easier form of communication than speaking. For Judy too, this became an intense activity – writing more letters to one person than ever before. For two somewhat lonely people, experiencing new emotions and deep spiritual uplift, the writing and receiving of letters became a daily 'life-line'. They were well written, often very long, and positive.

Packets of letters written 1956–61

The postal system was extremely good. A letter posted late in the evening at Bletchley could be sure of reaching a certain nurses' Home in the East End of London the next morning. They were eagerly written and joyfully received! Our Cupid wore the hat of a postman! By the end of 1957 Judy had written 175 letters to her air force sweetheart/university student! He had written 176!

Where did we find the time? – or the money for postage stamps? They say that 'love will find a way'. They were extremely busy times. My letters repeatedly report long shifts of work, particularly late in the day and into the night. During the Suez Crisis, in the autumn of 1956, it was nearly non-stop. I was very tired for much of the time. It was, however, not all work. I managed to travel by rail down to London to see Judy, using a cheap day return, once or twice a week.

Sometimes I would hitch-hike, using the A5 to north London when Judy was at home. Hitch-hiking-in uniform, of course – became my chosen method of travel for the long journey home to Bristol. Leaving camp at 5 pm, I was home by 9.30 pm with lifts via Aylesbury, Oxford, Cheltenham and Gloucester.

Judy was increasingly busy as her training progressed. There was much studying to be done during the initial three months. Thereafter, with exams passed in December 1956, it was ward work concentrating on various forms of treatment and age groups. The London Hospital had annexes in the Home Counties. Judy

Bristol reached after a long hitch-hike

spent three months at Banstead in Surrey and nine months at
Brentwood in Essex, where she did her theatre training. There, too,
she was near her beloved church at Southend which she could visit
easily. I had to change my travel plans to cope with these moves.
Banstead was reasonably easy. Euston was on the Northern Line
and terminated in Surrey at Morden. A bus then would take me
through Sutton to Banstead. One Sunday I arrived in time to go
to church with Judy. She was then on duty all the afternoon, so I
settled down to sleep in a field opposite the hospital – to be woken
by children playing nearby and telling one another that – 'there
was a dead man over there!'

Two important events during that autumn were to influence
our lives. Both of them involved our friend, George Bennett. The
first was his wedding to Christine on 15 September 1956.to which
I had been invited, chiefly because Judy was a bridesmaid. The
event passed off very smoothly and happily despite a degree of

North Yorkshire Moors with lorry sketch

sadness at the recent death of
his father. Judy stayed on near
York; I with Mrs Bennett at
Boston Spa. We had four days
of holiday, seeing as much of one
another as could be arranged.
Sunday took us to Christine's
Baptist Church in York-where
the minister Revd Davies greatly
impressed us. We had Sunday
Lunch with her parents when
proper Yorkshire Puddings were
served separately, before the rest
of the meal. Another day, we
went by bus to Knaresborough,

and then the most memorable was a day spent, with a picnic, up on the North Yorkshire Moors at Saltersgate. We were so engrossed in one another that we lost track of the time and missed the last bus back to Pickering. So, my thumb had to wag, to hitch a lift for two. We returned to London together where, after lunch, I was seated in an armchair when Judy, perched on its arm, tumbled into my lap, and we exchanged our first kiss! (and about time, too!)

Our letters of that autumn show how close we were growing, spiritually, physically and emotionally. We shared a sense of calling to God's work particularly in the overseas mission field. This continued to inspire our studies and training through a long engagement and into marriage. At that time, however, we felt a need for some act of commitment together, to cement this purpose in our lives. We decided to ask for Believers Baptism at the church in York. To be baptised together became meaningful for us both. Despite objections from our parents, we travelled to York to be baptised on the last Sunday of December 1956.

Morning QT

On the harbour wall

Family leaning on gate

In May 1957 I enjoyed my first holiday with Judy and her family. I went by train to the Methodist Guild Holiday at Treloyhan Manor near St Ives in Cornwall. It was my first visit to that beautiful corner of England. It was a first experience of Methodist Fellowship in holiday mood – at the house, in the gardens, at church (I even offered to preach a sermon!), on walks along the cliffs, and in self-made entertainment. On the final night, I dared sing a comic duet with Judy's mother! The Princes were able to call in to meet my parents in Bristol on their way home. I don't think they met again, until a certain wedding day four years later! Judy stayed a further week!

In the first week of September, my National Service came to an end, and I headed for the next stage of my life. Judy travelled to Bristol with me as we had both been invited to attend the wedding of Allan and Dorothy Barnes, at which. I was to be his best man.

I had much adjusting to make to civilian life, particularly in my financing. I was to live at home, so a contribution towards my keep was expected. I planned to give my parents £2 a week, then

Best man at Allan's wedding

10/ – for visits to London (once a month), 10/ – for savings and
10/ – for personal expenses. As to saving for the future, I was to
rely on what I could earn during vacations. Even before demob, I
had visited Bristol Temple Meads Station to arrange employment
as a parcel porter. This began during my first week of 'freedom'.

Judy and I were planning to become engaged at the end of the year.
We felt that we would cope better with the separations of the next
three years if our intentions were 'official'. So, the first three weeks
of working on the railway was designed to provide money for the
ring. I earned about £20 – the ring was to cost £18.

Chapter Four
Together At Last

UNIVERSITY YEARS

In October my life as a Bristol University student began. I was to study for a general honours degree in three chosen subjects, and a compulsory course in Latin or Greek. I chose Latin as in it I had an O-level pass. The subjects I really wanted to teach were geography, history, and English. In these subjects I was to be studying with 'specialist' students, so a high level of study was experienced in each. It was, after all, an honours course and one that I felt was best for a teaching career. It was a new life for me, having never been trained to study on my own before. Listening and noting lectures, attending seminars and tutorials were new experiences for me. In addition, I had had two years away from academic work whilst in the RAF. How wise it now seemed were those who had gone straight to university from school-especially since National Service, itself, was soon to end. My friend Roger was still completing his classics honours degree course at Oxford. He was to prove very helpful to me in my struggles with Latin during my first year at Bristol. I failed in Latin at the end of June and had to re-sit the subject in September before being allowed to continue. Roger and I worked together at Bristol Temple Meads for six weeks during the summer. 'Between trains' we would sit on a trolley and he would drill me in Latin grammar. The exam I took in September was the only exam I have ever left before time. I had finished, checked and rechecked

everything I had written! Soon, I learned that I had passed, and
could continue with the subjects that I wished to teach. Over thirty
years later, I found myself in a private prep school teaching – yes,
Latin! Thank you, Roger!

There was more to university than study. The societies and
clubs to join are legion – the danger lies in joining too many and
so doing less study. Besides them, there were activities at my home

Bristol University

church on Bedminster Down. At university I joined BIFCU –an interdenominational Christian Fellowship – thus continuing the type of meeting and thinking that I had enjoyed with SASRA. Through BIFCU I was to join in two missions during vacations, organised through the Inter Varsity Fellowship. Both were based at Baptist churches, one at Shoeburyness; the other at East Barnet. Both were in easier reach of a trainee nurse in London! They were interesting, learning experiences and helped me to realize that I

IVF Mission to Shoeburyness

should concentrate on my training to be a teacher. With this in mind, I followed, throughout my degree course, an extra activity designed to give to intending teachers, a qualification that would enable them to assist with games and gymnastics. This proved to be useful in both of my major schools.

Early in my first year, I attended the Toc H Lunch Club – a weekly gathering of hungry students to eat and listen to a speaker concerned in some social activity. I was interested in the practical Christianity shown in some of these, and became linked with the

Cotswold farmhouse – Dor Knap

work being done in the Toc H Hospital Broadcasts. These included Record Request programs for which I went round the wards of Bristol hospitals asking patients if there was a favourite piece of music they would like to hear. One request was to hear her canary singing which involved us in visiting her home in Clevedon to record the dear bird!

This link with Toc H was to continue into later years when I had started teaching. We had one weekend helping to renovate a Cotswold farmhouse above Broadway in Worcestershire. This became a conference centre and when visiting it as such, I enquired what use it was put to between weekends. 'None,' I was told. I then asked if I could bring a party of school children to stay for the four nights of a school week. So began a series of eleven Broadway Trips during my teaching at Churchill School. I shall tell more about them, later, in this my life of learning.

I played several games of hockey in university sides, but my main connexion continued to be with the Church Mixed Hockey Club.

Fancy Dress for Church Gala   Mum and Dad on holiday

The new vicar, Christopher Sutch, was a very good player and with his help we had considerable success. Weddings were usually held on a Saturday, and when Christopher gave a final blessing from the altar, you could see he had hockey socks on for that afternoon's game! There were some very good Mixed Hockey teams in the Bristol area and there were keenly contested cup matches.

At St Oswalds, I helped in the Sunday School which was all good practice for my intended career. Part of this, too, was the playing of the piano for the hymns, another 'skill' from my school days to be put to practical use. The preparation for Sunday school teaching was shared with Pam Richards, the young wife of Don, a naval officer, who was an old boy of QEH. We also played tennis, one of the games I was learning on the PE Course.

My university years were stressful at home on account of the deteriorating health of my father. Early in 1958 he developed a deep

infection of the small intestine. He lost weight rapidly until he was
but six stone. The hospital doctors seemed uncertain as to the cause
of his trouble. At one stage, infusions of suitable family blood were
suggested. Both John and myself made our first gifts of blood for
him. However, these had only a temporary effect, and in May 1959
Dad was admitted to the BRI for an ileostomy operation. They had
to build up his strength before this was possible. He was so thin.
Through all this time Mother lived in great stress as to the possible
outcome. Seeing her dear 'Hugh' in such pain and discomfort made
great demands on her faith, her own strength and her determination
to share his burden. I was glad that I was studying in Bristol and
living at home. She was, naturally, not always easy to live with. She
was very moody, and often refused to speak to me for a period of
days. Dad's operation meant that he would wear a colostomy bag
for the rest of his life. Nevertheless, he faced this handicap with
fortitude and remarkable cheerfulness. His recovery was steady
and his return home a great occasion. Two weeks convalescing at
Bournemouth, shared with Mum, gave them both new hope for the
future. Dad was to live for another twenty-eight years, outliving
Mum by thirteen years!

The next big event in my life was the completion of Judy's training
at the London Hospital in March 1960. Two months later she began
her midwifery training at Southmead Hospital and Mortimer House,
both in Bristol! So, our letter writing became a thing of the past. Now,
we could see one another with little difficulty or expense. Part of her
training was as a District Nurse in the Staple Hill and Downend areas
of the city. By that time, too, my own teachers' training had begun.
In June 1960 I succeeded in obtaining a 2nd class general honours
degree, majoring in geography, history and English. I was to teach
all three subjects at various times in my career, but when I enrolled
in the Bristol Education Department, I specialized in geography.

One of the attractions of the Bristol course was that there were no final examinations. Our ability to teach was measured by continual assessment, and for this, teaching practice was to be for a whole term – in the spring. I was directed to a comprehensive school at Lockleaze, Bristol. It was a secondary modern school that had just been upgraded to the comprehensive status (Bristol was leading in this development). The headmaster was determined to upgrade the appearance of his staff, too. He encouraged

Graduate

everyone to wear gowns. Mine was one of the newest! The resident geography teacher, Mrs Painter, was a great help to me. She said, 'I need not tell you what to teach. What I will do, is to teach you to cope!' This valuable ability has assisted me through all the changes to be experienced in the years ahead.

SEARCH FOR EMPLOYMENT

That year, 1961, was full of changes. Early in January, I had applied for the post of geography teacher at Churchill County Secondary School in the village twelve miles south of Bristol. I was invited to visit the home of the Headmaster, Reginald Dennis, one dark evening prior to my appearing before the School Governors at the school itself on 13 January. On my bus ride from Bristol to Churchill, I spotted a 'rosy-faced' farmer type occupying one of the seats. He was warmly dressed in coat and scarves. Later, as I viewed the two

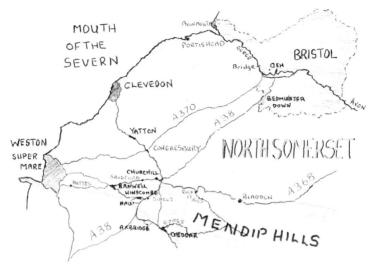

North Somerset

lines of governors either side of a long table in the staffroom, I was
surprised to see my 'farmer' among them. He was now to be seen
wearing a dog-collar! He was the local Methodist Minister, later to
become a good friend. The Chairman was a retired Colonel. He was
interested in my National Service and asked what of lasting value I
had gained from my two years in the RAF. I mentioned of course,
my fiancée nurse whom I was planning to marry in six months' time!
On being asked why I wanted to teach geography in their school,
I replied, pointing through the windows 'Look at those Mendip
Hills! Who wouldn't want to teach geography here?' On that Friday
the thirteenth I was offered my first teaching position, at Churchill
School – a post I was to hold for the next twelve years! Friday the
thirteenth has been my lucky day ever since! I went to the nearest
phone box to call Judy at Mortimer House, where that very day,
she had delivered a little girl whose home was in a village near to
Churchill. I met that girl many years later at the school, and she

Winscombe Hall in snow

was amazed when I told her that I knew the date of her birthday!

Having received the post, we started looking for our first home in that North Somerset area. The headmaster told me that the owner of a large house near Winscombe, Mr Gunn, was looking for a tenant for one of his lodges. I hurried to meet with this gentleman, but the lodge had been taken. Seeing my disappointment, he kindly offered me 'a suite of rooms' in a wing of his Winscombe Hall. The rent would be £2 a week, but we had to be responsible for the necessary decorating and furnishing of the three large rooms, kitchen, morning room and bathroom. He would pay for the materials used. Knowing that my parents were experienced home decorators, I accepted the challenge of preparing the Hall Flat to be our first home.

Much of the next five months was to pass before this was successfully accomplished. I was still completing my Education Year at Bristol University. (When asked what I was studying, I said, 'a paper on the Mendips'. I didn't mention that it was wallpaper!) The

Hall Flat lounge

Hall Flat windows   In my study

three large rooms were 11 feet 6 inches in height. A roll of wallpaper was used for three drops of paper from top to bottom. I would fix the upper 6 feet; then Mum would do the lower half. When Dad had a fall whilst painting a ceiling, Mr Gunn, then, insisted on employing a local man to help us.

My teaching at Churchill began sooner than expected, as the headmaster contacted the Education Department to ask that I be released from my course early to fill a vacancy at the school. So, I found myself teaching two weeks before my wedding, then away for two weeks honeymoon, followed by another two weeks until the end of term. We even received a wedding present from the staff!

TOGETHER AT LAST

We were married at Oakwood Methodist Church, North London on July 1st 1961. Roger Billings was my best man. The Princes' home

The bride crossing the road

The bride and groom

Bridal party

Over eighty guests

Judy's only time in the driving seat

was opposite the church, so Ron Prince simply walked his daughter across the road! There were over eighty family and friends to pack the church on one of the hottest days on record. Judy's sister, Catherine, was Bridesmaid with two little girls from the church in Southend to help her. The reception was held in the adjacent hall. The menfolk gave a cheer when Ron took his coat off!

He, later, drove us to Heathrow to enable me to board an aircraft for the first time. Maybe it was because of that, that I found I had a seat apart from my wife! Like so many others, we were spending our honeymoon in Jersey. We (non-smokers) were given an ashtray in the shape of the island during our two weeks holiday. On 2 July we attended morning service in St Aubin Methodist Church informing them that it was our first day of marriage. The following day we foolishly sunbathed on a nearby beach and were so burnt that we could hardly touch one another that next night! We hired bicycles for the length of our holiday with

Judy map reading

the aim of visiting all the parishes of the island. We also visited Guernsey during our second week. Little did we know then, of the place in our story that the Channel Islands were to have in years to come.

Chapter Five
My Teaching Career Begins

CHURCHILL COUNTY SECONDARY SCHOOL

So, began, then, our four years stay at Winscombe Hall. From there, I began my teaching career that was to last for twenty-nine years. School buses brought the children from the local villages to school each day. I began using the bus from Winscombe, but then Mrs Weir, a lady teacher, daily driving up the A38 close to the Hall, was able to pick me up each morning.

David Holt

David Holt was to be a special friend for thirty-eight years. He was the geography teacher whose position I was to fill in 1961 whilst he went off to finish his teaching qualification with an extra year of training. We met him and his wife, Margaret, in the January of my appointment. They helped us in the first searching for a home. They were moving from their rented flat to a permanent property, but their flat was not available to us. David returned to Churchill School in 1962, but by then I was established in the geography department. He was soon to move on to teach geography in the Wells Blue School. However, by then our friendship was firm.

Two developments were at the root of this. First, I decided that I should learn to drive. I started lessons with an instructor based in Winscombe. A little Austin 8 was for sale and I purchased this. Mr Gunn offered me a garage at the Hall for a further 15/ – a week. David was, by then, living in Sandford, a village very near to the school. We devised a plan. He kept my car in his garage and drove it each morning to school. I still had my lift with Mrs Weir and then, after school, I would drive my car (with David) home to the Hall. Each day I could practise the various handling requirements to pass the test. Through that autumn, I drove in almost all-weather conditions, so I was ready for the snowy winter that was to follow.

Hockey was the other interest we shared. David was a keen player in the Yatton and Cleeve men's team. Its home ground was at Cleeve. He invited me to join. It was quite a long drive to both home and away matches. Over coming years, we played teams as far apart as Weston Super Mare, Bristol and Trowbridge.

Judy began her midwifery work in September 1961 at the hospital in Weston Super Mare. The unit was small and badly needed a new trained midwife. Her hours had to fit with the local bus timetable. She caught the bus coming from Cheddar that dropped her just a short walk to the hospital. Midwives, I am told, look forward to part three of their training – which is to have a baby themselves! This was to begin in the spring of 1962 – maybe when we helped to lead our first Easter Holiday Fellowship at Towyn in West Wales, famous for its steam railway. The leader was another teacher at the school, Nick Livingstone, who taught art. He was to lead several similar holidays in the years to come.

THE ARCTIC ADVENTURE

But the greatest venture of that year, undertaken by that amazing secondary modern school was the expedition to Arctic Norway and

Norway–Finland expedition, 1962

Finland. It was the first such school to receive a grant from the Royal Geographical Society towards the cost of the venture. It was the science master, Alan Marsdon, who planned this extraordinary month for twelve senior boys and four masters to drive in three Landrovers to Newcastle, for shipment to Bergen; to Tromso by coastal steamer; camping and then driving deep into Finland; then trekking, carrying all their food, bedding and tents for ten days through the Tundra of Lapland; driving back to Tromso; and then for six days on rough roads, down to Bergen; by sea to Newcastle and then home to Somerset. It took most of August 1962 to complete, and many months previously, to prepare for it. The aftermath, involved me in compiling a report on the whole venture for presentation to those who had supported us. There were several places where I was required to speak and display the photographs taken and to show the film that was made.

That film was shown again when seven of those 'boys' met with one member of staff for a reunion, fifty years later in September 2012. We met at what is now Churchill Academy and were interested to learn that a party of senior students there, were planning a visit to Antarctica later that year. So, we must have started something, all those years ago.

DRIVING AND DELIVERING

The first two weeks of December have usually been momentous

Stories to tell, September 1962

.... and remember, September 2012

Baby Stephen dressed to go out

in our lives. In 1962 it could have been the birth of our first child or perhaps my passing of the driving test. On 10 December Judy had a medical examination at Weston Hospital, and was kept in. It had been arranged that I should attend the birth, if all was well. At 11 pm Mr Gunn, in nightwear, knocked at our door to tell me I was required at the hospital. I rode my bicycle furiously down to Sandford, demanded my car, and drove myself alone along empty roads to Weston. At 3.55 am on 11 December Stephen Martyn was born without complications. I saw his head first! So thrilled was I, that on my way home, I stopped to give a workman a lift to his work. I had to tell someone that I was a new father! I remember, too, that the hymn sung at school that morning was 'Unto us a child is born'!

Two days later, I took my driving test and passed first time. For the emergency stop, I was warned that the examiner would slap his book. Within seconds, a cyclist wobbled across my path and I slammed on the brakes. He never had to slap his book! I think, now, of the importance driving has been at various times in my life, and am grateful for my success that day, and for the help I had received from family and friends. One of my first drives was to meet Judy's Mum at Weston Station and take her home to meet her first grandson. Ron Prince came a little later to take Mum home for Christmas. On Boxing Day, it began to snow.

The schools were all closed, of course, but they were not to reopen for the Spring term for several weeks. The country roads and lanes were filled to their hedge tops. Even when we did reopen, the school coaches could not reach the school itself. We had to guide the children to the main road, which was cleared, and meet them there the next morning.

Churchill staff, 1963

TEACHING AT CHURCHILL

Since September, I had been using the official geography room. It was pleasantly situated at the end of one of the wings of the building. Through my training, I knew that visual aids were of supreme importance in the teaching of my subject. I began to build a store of pictures, maps, diagrams, film strips and transparencies for projection, Recordings of BBC Schools Broadcasts were extremely useful. Large pieces of rock decorated one side of the room, promoting an early interest in geology. I purchased a half-frame camera which enabled me to take seventy-two pictures on one roll of film. I became a great user of blackboards. Writing on them was a technique in itself. From my earlier letter writing, I developed a

style of hand writing suitable for chalk work. What did I write?
–mainly notes for later learning, questions and instructions. I still
had all my notebooks created in my own schooldays. The diagrams
and simple pictures found in them were to be used, sometimes, in
all my own teaching.

One feature of teaching at Churchill for me was that I found
myself working in a group of people of different ages. There were
some of a similar age to myself, but several others who were older

Staff take the leads in *HMS Pinafore*

and more experienced than me. Within the classroom one is alone,
but it was good to know that their other people around who could
advise, help and support me. They all became friends, sometimes
for life. In the room above me was Bill Brookes, teaching technical
drawing, with whom I coached and watched cricket. (he, even,
renewed my blood transfusion service!) The homes of these colleagues
also were to be part of our friendship. A number joined in the
annual operettas directed by Ray Miell and later myself. Charles
Leeming and his wife were Methodist friends; Tom Sherman, the

musical director, and Michael Hase who both introduced me to the Weston Operatic Society; also taking part was Heather Goodman who headed for the mission field before we did; Ann Hopes is remembered for hundreds of after-school cups of tea. Eddie Morgan, deputy head, was an unforgettable partner in the Arctic. Michael Bridge, a brilliant teacher of special needs children with whom I arranged class exchanges with similar children based at Lockleaze School. (Country children enjoying a week in the city; and then, in return, city children staying in homes in the country.) There were many more who joined the school in later years who could be mentioned. The point to be made, however, is that all these people were part of my learning experience for Life.

SCHOOL SHOP

A notable undertaking at Churchill was my school shop. Early on, I was surprised at the number of pupils who came to school without writing or drawing implements. With permission, I borrowed £5 from the school fund and bought a supply of pens, pencils, rubbers, and bottles of ink. (Biros were not encouraged in those days.) Over the years, my 'stock' multiplied in character and cost. As a child, I had often 'played at shop' much to the amusement of family and neighbours. This venture at Churchill School occupied my morning and dinnertime breaks. My initial £5 was soon paid off, then, over the years, as much as £2000 were raised for the School Fund. Some things were bought for School use. I bought cheap violins for which Tom Sherman would pay me 6d to balance the book. He had one very good violinist in the school, and other children wished to learn. I imported hockey sticks from Pakistan when I was introducing the game for boys. I sold seed potatoes and washing up liquid, sportswear and badges. The school decided to change its original blazer badge. We held a competition for a new

The school shop sold new Indian-style hockey sticks

design, and, when chosen, for a while I became the only supplier of
those badges. On 15 February 1971, our currency was decimalized.
For this, I was able to get, in advance, a supply of the new coins.
The children flocked to the shop to get their change in them. All
good learning for them, of course!

BROADWAY

I have mentioned my connection with Toc H at university,
and the renovated farmhouse at Broadway, Worcestershire. I was
to take second year pupils, both boys and girls on eleven visits to
Dor Knap as it was named. The first was actually only for boys
and Michael Bridge shared the lead. Thereafter, I had to persuade
a lady member of staff to care for the girls and to drive one of the
two hired buses. Later, the school owned its own bus. For many of
the children, this was their first holiday away from their Somerset
homes. Some needed instruction on making a bed! Some had not
slept with other children around them. There were six bedrooms,

Broadway trip, on top of Tewkesbury Abbey

Broadway trip, on top of Malvern Beacon

two for boys, two for girls, one for each of the staff. Tommy and his wife were the wardens, and they fed us splendidly throughout the week with breakfast and a cooked evening meal and a prepared mid-day picnic for wherever we went. I can recall no complaints or difficulties of behaviour.

The Broadway trip occupied a week of school time, so I tried to involve other subjects besides my own. Over the years, I learned of particularly interesting places to visit both from Dor Knap, and on the journeys to and from Broadway. Going, we visited Bath (the Costume Museum) and the American Museum. Up on the Cotswolds, with candles provided, we entered an ancient Iron Age barrow, and, sometimes, Prinknash Abbey near Cheltenham. On the return journey, we climbed the tower of Tewkesbury Abbey, after finding the abbot's tomb decorated with worms; then headed for the castle at Chepstow, and then over the new Severn Bridge before driving to their individual homes, for, by then, it was evening. A couple of places we always visited every year. A drive through Evesham took us to the Malvern Hills. On the Beacon they could see vast distances; on the Hereford Beacon were steep, Iron Age, grassy slopes, down which they loved to roll. Prior to the day, I would tell them how much Edward Elgar loved the Hills, and I even dared to play them 'Nimrod', and told them the music described 'the shape of the Hills'! The other 'must' place was the new Coventry Cathedral. We started in the old blitzed cathedral where I spoke about Reconciliation and the crosses of nails found in the burnt timber, and now made, to be sent to places all around the world. (Later, I found one in Napier Cathedral in New Zealand.) Then, with modern art in mind, we entered the new building. The children were set free to explore and be impressed by what they saw in window engravings and huge tapestries (Jesus with a small man at his feet) and all the treasures of that remarkable building.

Broadway trip:

Top left, the girls sliding down the earthworks at British Camp (Hereford Beacon).

Top right, the girls climbing up British Camp.

Right, boating at Malvern's Priory Park.

One boy, I remember, sought me out to tell me he had found 'the biggest fossil in the world' (he knew of my interest in geology). It was the huge shell carved within the font, made itself from a rock found in Galilee!

MOVING HOME

In 1965 we decided to move from Winscombe to Cheddar. We were helped by Judy's father to buy a new house, set in a quiet cul-de-sac with wonderful views of the famous gorge; with the cheese factory

The Font, the largest fossil in Coventry Cathedral

nearby. Several staff members lived in the village, too. My parents, also, moved that year from Bristol back to Weston Super Mare.

They found a home with Mum's sister, Nell, and it was there in 1966 that they awaited my return from the hospital where our second son, David James, had been born on 18 June.

With the sale of their house in Bristol my parents could, then, seek their final home in the growing village of Yatton. We

Mum with boys at Cheddar   Longwood cottage

became associated with the Methodist church in Cheddar. With a swimming pool in the village, Judy held events there to raise funds for missionary work. There Stephen was to learn to swim. Baby David drew a family gathering when baptized at our church there. Memorable, too, was a stormy night with a torrent down the Gorge and widespread flooding as a result. Stephen was old enough to start school there, before we made another move to the other side of the hills, to the village of Banwell.

LONGWOOD

Judy had always wanted to live in a cottage and this we found along High Street. It was named 'Longwood'. It was the first home our boys were to know. Stephen's room looked over the front gate and his railway occupied much of David's room.

His picture of 'a train of the future' was to win recognition in a Blue Peter competition. He was entertained at Bristol Temple Meads, and then on a joy ride to London. His picture was on display at Euston Station. Both boys were to attend school in Banwell. Judy continued with her midwifery in Weston Hospital until part three again occurred, and Timothy Paul was on his way. He was born on 16 August 1971 on the same bed as his brothers! He was the last child to be born to us. Ruth was yet to appear. We all attended the

Above, Stephen at Bristol Temple Meads.

Left, Baby Tim with Judy.

Banwell Methodist church. I enjoyed the choir there, as did David at a later date. We made many friends there who were to give us much support in the years ahead.

CHURCHILL SCHOOL BECOMES COMPREHENSIVE

Things were on the move, too, at Churchill School. Mr Dennis retired, and Mr Desmond Foster was appointed to guide the secondary modern school into being a comprehensive school taking in pupils

House block at Churchill School

of all abilities. It grew year by year-a new class being added each year. The fifth year would then be sitting CSE or Ordinary Level examinations, then going on to do Advanced Level for two further years in a sixth form. CSE was a new exam which involved teachers in its marking and grading – for which we were paid extra! Grading also gave me an opportunity to meet the geography teachers in other schools. This was a useful experience, as I was to find Indian schools very much tied to examination courses. As Churchill School grew, it first needed a Lower School in which these extra children were to be housed. The classrooms were open-planned. Teachers had to get used to working, with other classes, differently occupied, in the same area. The answer to that arrangement was worksheets! Under the guidance of Don Broughton, the Lower School head, I learned how to plan and write worksheets. He would read each draft through, as 'the idiot child in the class' – pointing out what he did not understand or follow. I enjoyed the challenge of this, and contrived other ideas to add to the sheet. For example, I compiled crosswords with clues that the youngsters could solve by reading books or looking at maps or pictures. I found myself teaching English and history in the Lower School, too. Two house blocks were then constructed with a new geography lab on the upper floor of one of them. Two rooms could be used for teaching, so we now had a geography department, which, in turn, needed a head of geography! Unknown to me, an advertisement for this person had been placed in the Educational Press. I made an application for my job, as I thought it, just before my annual visit to Broadway with second year pupils. The interviews were set for that very week when I would be away. Some kind person came up to Dor Knap to take me back for them, but I failed to get 'my job.' A younger, fitter man was appointed. He had already been teaching A Level at a grammar school in Bristol. Being the Captain of the Bristol Rugby Union Club might also have helped him. He was to leave the school six months after I had done so.

Chapter Six
Mount Hermon Calls

MISSION CALLING

Judy and I had for many years been involved in the Overseas Missionary work of our churches. This was the dream-the longing – that had initially brought us together in 1956. All Judy's training and work experience had been to make her equipped for work overseas. I, too, early in our relationship, realised that I wanted to teach alongside her. I even mentioned this intention in my speech to family and friends as a newly married husband! Wisely, we decided that we needed five years of practical experience in our callings; I became a full-time teacher at Churchill School. Judy was a welcome Midwife at the Maternity Unit at Weston Hospital. She, however, kept practising her part threes! Stephen, David and Timothy were spaced well apart in their arrivals in 1962, 1966 and 1971. After David's birth we did start to investigate the possibilities of work overseas. We became Prayer Partners of BMMF (the Bible and Medical Missionary Fellowship). In their annual Prayer Handbook, we were interested to see missionary family photographs in various parts of the Indian sub-continent. Clearly children were catered for! At the rear of the book was a list of the addresses of the missionaries supported. They welcomed the receipt of letters from interested people. We wrote to several places where we knew there were schools. We had decided to find a teaching post, thinking there would always be nursing jobs nearby. We applied to Lushington

School at Ootacamund in Tamil Nadu; to Woodstock School in Landour, and to Dr Graham's Homes in Kalimpong. In these there were no openings for a geography teacher.

DARJEELING

Soon after Tim's birth, the changes at Churchill School made us 'test the water' again for another try for overseas work. This time, I wrote to Dorothy Barker, working in language translation in Darjeeling – a hill station in which there might be schools. She wrote back to say there were two Christian schools. St Pauls was the 'Eton of the East,' as she called it; and Mount Hermon, a co-educational school with an evangelical Christian bias. I wrote to both, and the principal of Mount Hermon replied saying they were losing their geography teacher in 1974, and would be interested in my replacing her. He and his wife were to visit the UK early in 1973 and would be glad to visit us at our family home in Banwell. On the Friday evening at the end of my last Broadway trip, there they were, armed with photographs of their family and school, and willing to answer our questions. Stephen, as we knew he would, asked about snakes. Graeme Murray told him he had only seen six in all the years he had been there! They, further, won Stephen over when they showed him pictures of the Darjeeling Himalayan Railway!

Soon after that visit we received confirmation from Darjeeling that we would be expected in that far away place in February of the next year.

This move was to affect the lives of several members of our family. My parents were dismayed to learn that three of their grandchildren were to be taken so far away. Long gone, were Mum's dreams of me becoming an Anglican priest, who might have, actually, sought work overseas. However, they decided, together, to support us in this new venture. As sincere Christians, they would find a part to play in this, as they gained knowledge of what our future work might actually be like.

They would be supported on the 'home front' by my dear brother, John. To him fell the responsibility of caring for the welfare of our parents. He and his wife, Joyce, had two teenage children when we left England. I soon came to realize that I could not have worked so long in India, without the tremendous commitment by them both.

LEARNING TO TRAVEL

From the Autumn half-term in 1973 we entered a time of life when we were to continue learning new things every day. I intend to label many of these 'things' or events LATT ie. Learning all the time. The first of these involved Luggage –all we needed to take for living and working in India. So, there was sea luggage; air luggage and hand luggage. We used Pickfords, of course, you might say.

They supplied us with eight tea chests (how appropriate for Darjeeling!), and also took large electrical items – -like a new Baby Belling cooker, refrigerator, washing machine, Flatley Drier, record player, tape recorder etc. away to be packed in a very large crate made of new, seasoned wood (of great use for months to come), and which was certainly dropped at least once on its journey.

Judy remembers packing tea chests in the living room at 'Longwood' as she watched a Royal Wedding on 14 November on television. In them she might have put books, records, blankets, sheets, big toys like Tim's Cyclops bike, crockery, kitchen ware and board games. We had been advised to stuff all holes with toilet paper which was not of good quality in India. (LATT). By the end of November, the sea luggage was on its way. We then turned, after Christmas, to the air luggage for flights in the second week of February 1974. With the hand luggage, this amounted to sixteen pieces. The last of them was a French Horn owned by the eldest son of the Revd Jones, (vice-principal of the school.) It had been taken in a damaged state to the repair shop of Boosey-Hawkes in London. I was asked to pick up this item, in its case, on my journey to the Airport. The repairers proudly showed me their beautiful repair, but my response was somewhat lacking, as I had never seen the instrument before! I decided that it should be Stephen's hand luggage. He was worried for fear that the Customs people might ask him to play it! This taught us to be careful about agreeing to carry other people's items. Latt. The Revd Bill Jones was able to help us with carrying a lost rucksack from Delhi a year later. He, also, taught Judy, on a visit to his home, how to open and eat mangoes. Latt for her!

We flew with Iraqi Airways as cheaply as possible (the school was to repay us). The journey had six stops: Paris, Athens, Bagdad, Bahrein, Karachi and New Delhi. There the immigration officer, on hearing me say, 'I have three children – all boys, I'm afraid,' leaned over his desk, shook me by the hand, and said, 'Congratulations, sir, on having three sons!' It was a Latt moment never to be forgotten! Next day, we flew on to Calcutta and then on to a flight for Bagdogra, learning only then that luggage weights are less on inland flights. Help was at hand. A governor of

the school, a leading politician of a Christian State we had never heard of, was travelling that day. He saw us through for the asking. (Latt again). Stephen Lewis, a good friend in the years ahead, met us at the airport with school transport. The drive up to Darjeeling took about five hours. The railway

Stephen's Garden DHR (many years later)

ran alongside the road for much of the way, and our Stephen had his first viewing of the steam train that was to be part of his life from that day onwards!

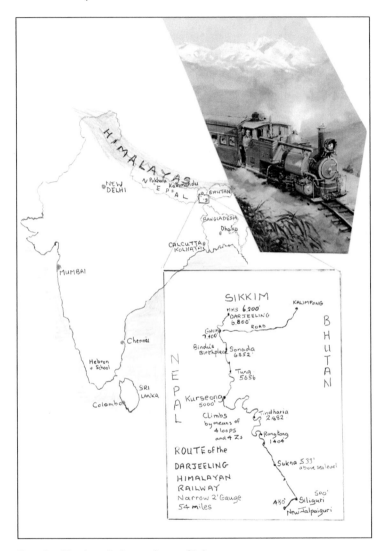

Darjeeling Himalayan Railway with map of India

Mount Hermon School, front view

MOUNT HERMON SCHOOL

So, on 12 February 1974 we began fifteen years of service at
Mount Herman School, (MHS) in the town of Darjeeling. It
had been founded in 1895 by American Methodists, to meet the
needs of girls and young boys of missionaries in India, and of local
Planters in the expanding tea industry. In 1926 the school moved
to North Point, where the impressive main building was erected. It
grew to become a complete co-educational, boarding establishment
for students from the age of five to eighteen. There is also a junior
school teachers college founded in 1964 within the campus, as are
the houses for staff. Before our arrival we were sent the prospectus
for the school. I quote from it here: 'It was founded as being a
Christian Institution in the Evangelical Protestant tradition.' It
has a motto: 'Not for school but for life we learn'.

From this, I take the title for what I am now writing. I quote
again:

So the School seeks to prepare a student not merely to pass examinations or enter a profession, but, also, to go out into the world equipped in body, mind and spirit to lead a full and useful life, satisfying to oneself, and of true value to the Community and Country, to Man and to God.

These words confirmed in us and my parents a sense that this truly was the place where God intended us to work. Our dreams of a 'bonga-bonga' land had turned out to be a place of mountainous beauty, surrounded by tea, and boys and girls eager to learn, and to love their school as much as we still do.

On the very first morning after our arrival at MHS, we saw Kanchenjunga, the third highest mountain in the world, within the Himalayas that dominate the skyline to the North of Darjeeling. The peak is forty-seven miles away, so looking not much higher than big mountains much closer to us. The 'snows' as they are called, are not always to be seen and hardly ever in the monsoon season, from May onwards, when most of Darjeeling's 400 inches of rain fall. The tea bushes love it, though!

Kanchenjunga across the playing field

Our skill at letter writing during our courting days again came into practice as we kept in weekly touch with our parents at home. Those letters have survived and reading their tiny writing brings to mind the challenges we had to face especially in the early months of our settling in. Occasionally, we might use quotations from these letters in the course of our story. Usually, at least one member of the family was feeling poorly. Sometimes three or four

Our bungalow Wattle

were suffering. Our bungalow, Wattle, (originally the property of an Australian mission) had been newly built after earthquake damage. It showed the problems of most such houses. It was cold; the chimney smoked; rainfall revealed leaks in the roof. The furniture was hard – particularly our bed! But we survived by gradually receiving help from the maintenance department, and from kind neighbours lending bedding and other items until the sea luggage arrived. John and Pauline West, our nearby English missionary neighbours, were particularly helpful. They became interesting friends. We were amazed how well our boys adapted to their new lives, even before the long-awaited sea luggage arrived. What a day that was! It was five months later, in June, seven months exactly, since it had left Longwood! One tea chest was delayed; the big crate of electricals had been dropped, damaging most of the items inside, but all but one was in working condition. They all needed round pin plugs for Indian connection. Latt.

JUDY SPEAKS

A month before we left England, we received a letter from Joyce Wainwright. She had recently left MHS and wished to recommend her ayah, Didi, to us. It was the first time I had realized that we would be expected to employ a servant. Didi presented herself to us on our very first morning. She had a letter from Joyce in her hand. She came each morning that week, and when our bungalow was ready for occupation, she came at 7 am to cook breakfast, cleaned the house whilst the tough meat cooked all morning, served dinner, and then went to her home high up near the HMI, (Himalayan, Mountaineering Institute) the home of Sherpa Tensing of Everest fame.

We didn't expect her to return in the afternoon as other servants were expected to do. We had a problem in paying her. When first we did so, she made no response. We wondered if we had not given her enough. We asked our new friends, John and Pauline West. 'Did she receive the money with both hands?' we were asked. We hadn't noticed. Next week, we observed. She, gratefully, received it

Judy with our Ayah, Didi

Judy with Shova at Hayden Hall

with both hands! Geoff would say that was a LATT moment. We ourselves began to receive with both hands, too!

We had much shopping to do. John West took us into Darjeeling first to just look around, noting especially the best places to shop. He said it was best to use places where we were known to be resident foreigners rather than tourists. On the second trip in the school jeep, we bought essentials for the new home – curtain material, a kerosene cooker, and kerosene itself, one large rug for the living room and two smaller rugs for the boys' bedrooms.

I was learning of the medical facilities in the area. I had visited the school infirmary with its twenty beds. In Darjeeling, there was Planters Hospital to be used by our Staff and boarding students. Then there was the Sadar Hospital which our servant community might use, supported by the school. They could get out – patient help at the School Infirmary, but I could see their need for a separate clinic. The local Jesuits had plans for building a new Welfare Centre, Hayden Hall, in the town. When I heard that they were planning to have a maternity wing, I immediately made contact. I started helping in their dispensary for two mornings each week. They also had an under-fives programme, where children were weighed, fed and, occasionally, given baths! I also went, with the Nepali Sister, to one of the local villages to attend the children there. There were delays in the erection of the main building due to a lack of funding from Canada. When it was finally opened, the Maternity section was scaled down and then abandoned after only a few months, again because of money problems.

However, the experience of helping at Hayden Hall was invaluable for my main work at MHS. At the end of our second year, Graeme Murray and Dr Pemba of Planters Hospital suggested that I should run a clinic for the servants and their families. An old greenhouse was converted for my use and I opened the clinic at the beginning of 1976. It was arranged that our Didi should be employed to help

Judy at MHS Servants clinic

me. This was necessary to help me with the language. Although I had some Nepali lessons from our Language staff, I was far from fluent. In the clinic we gave medicines for minor ailments, did dressings and injections (which I taught Didi to do). More serious illnesses were referred to the doctor at the Sadar Hospital in town. My emphasis was on the Maternity work and looking after the under-fives, giving immunizations against diphtheria, whooping cough and tetanus. In later years I was able to get the Polio vaccine, and arrange for someone to come from the municipality to vaccinate against smallpox and TB. We had a big anti-TB campaign which involved taking over three hundred servants and children into Hayden Hall for x-rays – and some for subsequent check-up and treatment.

I was occasionally called to the homes of the servants for a delivery or other emergencies. Sometimes I would need to take the patient into hospital. For this, the school provided its jeep (and driver). I would, afterwards, visit the mother and baby at home-using my portable scales donated by Methodist folk back in Banwell.

We also had a feeding programme when Dried milk and biscuits provided by the Red Cross would be given to about one hundred children coming to the clinic each day. I had help for this from students, and,

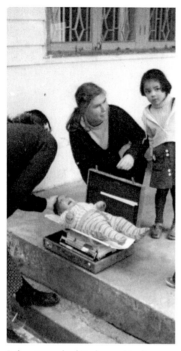

Judy using scales (Bindu watching)

for a while, from Hindi speaking Staff ladies who came to the clinic to give talks on hygiene etc .to the mothers.

During our years at MHS, several members of staff had babies, and I always got involved, though I never actually delivered one! I would go to the Planters Hospital with the mother and stay with her, sometimes overnight. Post-delivery, I would visit mother and baby at home (with my scales) and give any help as necessary.

MUM STOPS WRITING

Mum's letters to me through the first eighteen months of my time in Darjeeling were a mighty act of love to me. As soon as she had posted a letter to me, she began the next. So, each letter grew day by day. Then, a letter might arrive from me (I wrote each week) and she would begin to answer it immediately. So, at the end of her week, a six – or seven-page letter would be heading eastwards from the post box opposite her house! When I went home in December 1975, I found her next letter to me started, but never finished. She died of a heart attack on 4 September. John's telegram reached the school on the fifth, telling me that 'Mum passed peacefully away today. God bless'. Graeme Murray saw the telegram first, among a batch of other telegrams. He sent it, with a note, to Judy – as she would be the best to break the news to me. He and Patricia came that evening to visit us at home. Lovely people, both!

To my amazement, the next week I received a letter from my dear Dad. He said that he would try to write to me 'in place of your dear Mum'. And he did so, until his own death thirteen years later! I used to read his letters to the boys in a rich West Country voice, much to their amusement. On my own home visit that year, I discovered that Mum had been making cloth toys, ready for stuffing, for children. I took them back to India, and, gradually each found a home – the last one in our own home – a camel known as Oggie.

Chapter Seven
Life at Mount Hermon

TEACHING AT MOUNT HERMON SCHOOL

I had never before taught in a school like Mount Hermon. The nearest in my experience was QEH in Bristol, which was also a boarding school. At MHS, I had to understand the daily routine of the boarders. The girls' dormitories were on the third floor of the Main building; the boys' hostel was 200 yards down the hillside! They were all expected to attend morning study in the main building at 6.10 am for an hour's study before breakfast at 7.15 am. This was followed by chapel assembly; three lessons; recess (fifteen minutes) then two lessons:

View from the Stewart Building

lunch (forty minutes): three lessons until 2.35; tea (twenty minutes): sports (two and a half hours); 5.25 pm afternoon study (one hour); dinner 6.30; night study 7–8 pm: dormitories lights out 9 pm.

So, they had three hours of study Monday to Friday, with just morning study and four lessons on Saturdays. From all this, I realized that the provision of study notes was vital in their education. They were unhappy

Teaching from the *Western Mercury*

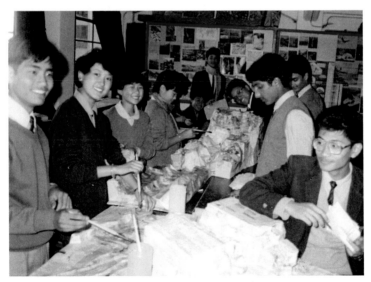

Landscape modelling

if they did not have copious notes to read and record. Most of my teaching took place in Stewart Building. What I wrote clearly on a blackboard was important to them. Often, of course, this included diagrams, maps and drawings which were all part of my method of teaching geography. The room had large blackboards and a movable screen. If I projected a picture, I could then move the screen and chalk the outline of the picture on a clean blackboard behind it for the students to copy and any notes I might add around it. There were big notice boards down one side of the room. I had plenty of pictures to display. The photo shows a copy of the *Weston Mercury* newspaper, above which are photos of Moorlands Guest House, the home of David and Margaret Holt, which the class are 'visiting' on a tour round the world! They, each, made a brochure for the house which our friends enjoyed seeing when I next went home. David, himself, was to visit the school in 1977, so the students met him then, when he thanked them for their hard work!

ISC students in geography were expected to present practical items from their studies. I had them making models of landscape features like river valleys and volcanoes, using torn paper, paste, and papier Mache, suitably painted when dry.

I also taught English to the classes preparing for the ICSE exam at the end of Class 10. They all had to pass in English to gain a certificate. This involved me in a mass of marking. Essays or compositions took ten to fifteen minutes each. I found it best if I could mark them alongside the student. I sometimes did this when I was on day duty. Mistakes could be pointed out, and praise given for good writing and ideas. Sometimes, what they wrote was inspired by a magazine picture I had given them individually. I used to mark these by reading them aloud to my children as bedtime stories! Teaching English literature for ISC (for classes 11 and 12) was a big challenge. The set books were often very difficult to

English literature class 12

Marking and report writing at home

understand, especially by Asian students. *Murder in the Cathedral* took us to twelfth-century Canterbury, and to Dickens' London in *Our Mutual Friend*. I enjoyed teaching Shakespeare for ICSE in classes 9 and 10. I brought recordings of the plays from England so that they could hear them spoken by real actors. Poetry, too, became enjoyable for both teacher and students. If they had been very good, sometimes, I would read 'The Highwayman' at the end of the lesson.

Swimming gala

JUDY TELLS OF HER ACTIVITIES

I became involved in lifesaving. Every summer (after the monsoon rains had filled the pool!) I ran classes for senior students based on the Royal Life-Saving Scheme for which Graeme Murray was an examiner. We obtained from them the official awards, but after he left, we based our own scheme on that of the RLSS, and had the badges made in town. In my last two years I trained some of the most senior students to be instructors in the hope that life-saving would continue. Also, in the swimming season, I undertook supervision duties – as all swimming had to be supervised.

I, also, taught students first aid as part of their SUPW (Socially Useful and Productive Work). I gave similar lectures to the college students, too. One year I took needlework classes, and even French to my own children when we lost our French teacher. Once or twice, I became a temporary matron in the little girls' dormitory, even living there on one occasion. Some of the dormitories and classrooms (pictured) were badly damaged in a later earthquake

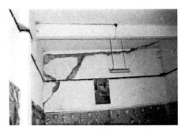

Classroom earthquake damage, 1988!

Manju – heading for Switzerland

One winter I spent three months at a Mission Hospital down on the Plains, one hundred miles west of Calcutta, 'working' in the maternity department. It was an interesting time, although I didn't do as much practical midwifery as I would have liked. However, I did achieve two deliveries and gave anaesthetics on four occasions.

In 1977, my work at Hayden Hall finished, and I was not so much needed at the infirmary. So I had a crèche at home for a few of the servants' children, to enable an elder sister to go to school. Also, a little girl, Manju, the daughter of an unmarried ayah, who we learned was up for adoption. This prompted us to make enquiries, but she had already been promised to a couple in Switzerland. So, we turned to the Mother Theresa Home in Darjeeling, and found Bindu.

BINDU

We knew that Dr David Goodall and his wife, Jackie, stationed at the Sarenga Hospital where Judy had spent some months, were in the process of adopting a little orphan girl left in the hospital. This encouraged us to act similarly. We were warned that the

Shishu Bhavan in Darjeeling received many disfigured babies. Nevertheless, on Friday 13 May (!) 1977 we set off to visit the home. Stephen, being fourteen years old, came with us. We were shown a little boy with no arms. We explained that we were hoping for a baby girl. There were plenty of them, the one we were shown had a mole on her forehead. She was a child of about sixteen months, and had been left in their care about a

Bindu comes home to Wattle   year earlier. Stephen had turned away and had left us. I hurried after him and asked him what was wrong. He didn't like that 'thing' above her eyes, but didn't object 'if we really wanted her.' Meanwhile, Judy was suggesting a method of removing the mole – with a thread tightened. When Judy first brought Bindu home a month later, Stephen took a quick look at her and said, 'Where's that thing?'

'Oh! It fell off,' he was told. Stephen, who already had painted a wooden cot a bright red for his new sister, loved her, as we all have loved her ever since.

Then, we had to prepare for a hearing at the Darjeeling Court in

order to gain legal guardianship
of Bindu, and permission to
take her to England at the end
of the year. We were guided by
a lawyer in this. We first had
to show that we had tried to
contact Bindu's mother. Visits
were made to her village. Letters
were written to her, returned
by the Post Office, 'addressee
unknown'. 'Hangings' in her
village, requesting information,
were made. The Sister from the
Shishu Bhavan attended the
hearing to explain Bindu's life
so far, and also, when asked,
assured that a home would be
there, if we were unsuccessful.

Stephen carries her on a walk

Our lawyer muttered to me that
he thought that was the way it
was going. I asked him to gain
permission for me to speak to
the judge. This was granted.
He was uncertain because I
had no teaching appointment
arranged for my return. Judy
said that, actually, she had work
promised at Weston-Super-Mare
Hospital – her salary might
have been more that the judge
himself received! So, to quote his

Bindu's Indian passport photograph

summary, he felt able 'to allow the application, more particularly, on the assurance given before me by Mr Blackmore, that this unfortunate girl will not be neglected.' This is why I have always felt that it was I who had delivered the fourth child of our family!

A DAUGHTER AT LAST, JUDY CONTINUES

There was much to be obtained to enable Bindu to travel to the UK .-a medical report on her health; a photo for her Indian Passport; consular approval for her visit to the UK in order to be adopted, and, of course, the actual passport. Mr Sarkar, of American Express Calcutta, was the man who did this for us. He, dramatically, withdrew it from his desk

Bindu helping at Longwood

drawer as being 'the greatest achievement in his life'. The main difficulty for him was caused by the absence of a Police Report on the criminal record of this little child! We rewarded him with yet another colourful tie!

The adoption process in the UK was simpler. For three months our home was checked by Social Welfare Officers. With our boys, we then had to appear before a judge 'in his chambers', where the boys, too, were questioned. So, Bindu became our adopted daughter on 12 June 1978. She had no birth certificate, but being four months old when her mother left her with the sisters in 1976, we estimated April to be her birth month and

Bindu marching with KG

made her birthday to be the twenty-first, in celebration of the Queen's Jubilee in the year that we found her. On 1 October she was baptized 'Bindu Ruth' in the Methodist church in Banwell where we were living. On the fifteenth of that month she was accepted as a British citizen.

Her new parents, however, were in the process of planning a return to India. With them and two of her brothers, she returned to the land of her birth in April 1979. Stephen, then settled for O- and A-level studies

at Churchill School, was found a home with church friends, Albert and
Ruby Russell in Banwell, and later in Loxton.

Our return to MHS in 1979 proved to be important for our little
daughter, Bindu. She celebrated her third birthday in April, and
Oggie was one of her presents. Sleep was impossible at night unless
she was holding 'the creature' that her grandma had made! Two years
later she was entered into the kindergarten class at school – a group
of little girls and boys, one of whom she was to marry twenty-seven
years later! When she became engaged to Rajan Shrestha, she told
us that they had been 'sweethearts' in KG!

MHS had, by then, become a school linked to preparing students
for Indian based examinations. These were of little use to our own
boys. Stephen was to remain in the UK from 1977 onwards to take
O and A levels at Churchill School. David was to spend some years
at Hebron School in Ootacamund South India to take O-levels
there before returning to Weston Technical College for training
in Catering and Hotel Management. He was to gain employment
at the Barbican Hotel in London, from whence he was invited to
join the staff at the Savoy Hotel. Tim also did O-levels at Hebron
and then joined Filton College at Bristol for business studies and
A-level economics to gain entrance to Guildford University to
finish with a degree in economics. Further training was to equip
himself with an accountancy qualification. Bindu was to spend just
eighteen months at Hebron School in preparation for schooling
in the Channel Islands.

Chapter Eight
Musical Life at Mount Hermon

What other activities, besides teaching, was I involved in right through my time at MHS? The first was singing. In the first year, 1974, the school had an excellent choir. I was happy to be allowed to take part, singing with the tenors. That senior choir was good enough to be invited to sing both in Calcutta and in Shillong, the capital of Meghalaya. They sang in schools, churches and even in Calcutta Cathedral. Sometimes the concert would be full of religious music; sometimes it would be more secular. The arrival of our sea luggage brought our store of records. Amongst them was one of Ralph Harris' songs. I equipped myself to sing his 'Jake the Peg' – needing to be sung with

Jake the Peg

Junior choir card

'his extra leg'. I lost count of the number of times I sang it! The school placed an emphasis upon singing. There was an intermediate choir and a junior choir, which I was to lead for a number of years towards the end of my time there. I encouraged each junior to have a

membership card, marking the practices and performances made on
Sundays. Bindu was in that choir, and her card has survived. There
were inter-house music contests, in Western music one year, and then
Asian music the next. The furore with which those contests were
prepared for and presented was amazing. The songs were chosen
by each house, and costumed appropriately. There was also a set
piece which each house sang. It was, usually, a hymn, and when that
hymn might later be selected for a service in chapel, the singing
was marvellous, with the four-part harmony still remembered. In
1984, with my son David's help, I made a tape recording of selected
music from the past ten years. I named it *Now's the Time for Fun
and Laughter*, words from one of the Going Home Day Songs. I
made a second tape after 1985/6 *Let Songs Be Blended* (after one of
the Going Home Day songs!), and a third 1987/8 *Sing Hallelujah!*.
Later, as CDs, they were popular mementos for many at reunions.

Conducting Junior Choir at Christmas Service

MAJOR PRODUCTIONS

On my CDs are many extracts from Major Productions (MP). With a couple of productions at Churchill behind me, I volunteered to direct musical MPs. On their visit to UK in 1972, the Murrays had seen *Fiddler on the Roof* in York. It was the last show I had been in with Weston Operatic. So, with my memory filled with the way it was directed, I was able to produce something memorable on the MHS stage in 1974. That MP was their choice, but I was, subsequently,

King & I wives in Western dresses

to find the actual choosing of each MP very challenging. I felt that it should have a story with a message for Life, dealing with real life situations. It should also be suitable for our students to present; even to the costumes they should wear. The Jewish refugee difficulties in *Fiddler*; the dependency on the traditions in their family lives; and in dealing with others who are different from themselves, were all factors that might occur in the students' own experience. So, in *The King and I* and the position of the monarch, needed

Judy makes eighteen kilts for *Brigadoon*

care in presentation because we had Thai students within the school. Many of the MPs had reference to the history of the people; to their ancestors who might appear as ghosts. Tevye is visited by his mother-in-law; *Scrooge* is visited by four ghosts with a remarkable change in his life; in *Ruddigore*, the pictures of ancestors come to life with great effect: in *Carousel*, Billy is lifted to the stars to be given another chance to change things below; and finally in *Brigadoon* most of the cast are ghosts because of their history!

Why did I like to direct the MPs? I would like to answer that with a comment made in my photo book by one of the principals of 'Summer Song'. 'Thanks a lot for all you've done for me. You've helped me gain more confidence in myself in a few months than I had gained in sixteen years.'

I preferred musicals because they involved a much larger number of students, usually a hundred or more. A straight play might use about thirty. But a musical has a team of principals; a large chorus of boys and girls, sometimes separated; there might be an off-stage chorus, too. There might be an orchestra of students and staff, led by the musical director, usually on the piano; the stage crew, directed by a manager (one of whom was an expert at making properties like binoculars and bagpipes); and then the lighting crew, high above the left wing of the stage. Also, I must not forget the back-stage team, busy at make up, costume making and prompting.

It was a tremendous operation, far bigger than anything I had tried to do previously. It was all done, usually, from two books: *The Musical Score* and *The Libretto*. The first task was the typing and duplicating of the words for each principal. (Thank you, RAF!) Then the whole action had to be planned or plotted, scene by scene. A plot had to be made for the stage crew to know where all the properties should go. Also, a lighting plot for them up there.

Amahl singing with Mrs Murray

Costumes had to be found, bought, adapted from a former MP, or completely new-made, like the Western dresses in the *King and I*, and the eighteen kilts for *Brigadoon* men made by Judy. Much depended on the cooperation of other members of staff and the maintenance department who built the scenery.

Each MP was different in its own particular way. It was planned to take *The King and I* to Kalimpong for a performance at Dr Graham's Homes, so the scenery had to be portable, for transporting forty miles over the hills, along with the cast and their costumes. Amongst them were children from North East India who looked Siamese for the school scenes. Older Thai girls sang their own songs as they danced in the manner true to their homeland. In the busy year of 1975, the MP became part of the Christmas Carol Service held in November. We did *Amahl and the Night Visitors* in which the major parts were the three kings and the mother of Amahl, her crippled son. It is an operetta without dialogue. The music is in solos, duets, and choruses, linked with recitative. Turbaned, I was one of the kings – the oldest and the most deaf! Patricia Murray was a fine mother, and a young girl took the part of Amahl.

Later in 1976 I directed the college boys and staff in *Trial by Jury*. It was preceded by a session of Call My Bluff between two teams of staff. It was chaired by Judy's father, Ron Prince, who was visiting the school with her mother. It proved to be a sad time though, as the lovely home of the Murrays was destroyed, one night, by fire. With the aid of a small photo I managed to paint a picture of their house, Elkanah. I also collected broken china from the site to decorate a large vase. Both items I have seen in their house in New Zealand.

The year 1977 saw the college boys again in action, this time with the ladies of Loreto College and our own staff. *The Gondoliers* brought forth some fine singing. Bronwyn Murray played the piano whilst her mother sang the duchess. It's the drummer who gets the prize of her daughter at the triumphant ending. I was happy to play that modest part!

I had limited experience of acting. No one had ever taught me drama. Early on, I bought the book *Play Production* by Henning Nelms which covered every aspect of directing and staging a play. The stage at MHS has an apron about a yard deep with steps leading down into the audience and to a side door. To rehearse scenes with large numbers, I sometimes decided to move aside the benches in

the Hall, so that an area the same size as the stage was exposed.
I could then direct the action of everyone without continual use
of the steps.

The back stage was the realm of the stage crew; above were the
lighting crew, who had more to do than just moving switches. One
of the spot lights could only be reached by crawling through the
ceiling above the audience. These hidden members of the mp team
had such an important part to play. The control and directing of

Painting of Elkanah

the lights were vital in gloomy, ghostly scenes of the drama. In
'fiddler' some of the cast held hand torches below their chins when
a ghost was screaming!

No microphones were used. Those were the days when actors and
singers really had to project their voices. Ours was a big hall and I
had to teach what I myself was only learning at the time. First, was
their position on the stage. Use the apron section wherever possible;
then to the directing of your words. Imagine a deaf old man (often

Top, stage crew with bearded director and prompt

Above left, applying makeup to juniors in the Green Room

Above right, Firdaus in her class play wearing an imported wedding dress!

Left, thank you card from a senior class.

me!) sitting in the back left-hand corner of the rising seats at the rear of the audience. Use the wall to your left to bounce your voice towards the rear of the hall. At night, avoid facing the curtained windows on your right. Entertain the audience; live the character you are assuming, if they laugh, wait before you next speak, they might laugh even louder!

I was concerned in the provision of costumes. Their storage was in what was wrongly called the Green Room. There was a good supply of costumes from previous events and plays. I was able to multiply their number by visiting Jumble Sales on my regular visits to England in winter. The Music Room at the rear of the stage had a row of cells for instrument practice. These were used by the male characters dressing for their play. The girls could easily use their dormitory upstairs. Make up was applied in the Music Room. Many of the costumes were for the junior classes preparing for

Maria's wedding in *The Sound of Music*

their class and chapel plays. I supplied them in baskets, and the Green Room walls became covered with thank you cards made by the classes afterwards.

I spent 1978 in England but returned to MHS the following year when a straight play was produced. The MP in 1980 was my next effort: it was *The Sound of Music*. This was dominated by principals. The mixed chorus only sing once, before the Von Trapp children wish them 'Goodnight!' The girls' chorus were first seen as nuns, wearing the habits loaned to us by the Sisters of a local convent school. Our new American music teacher, Sara Baraily, replacing Mrs Murray, had a fine voice for the Mother of the Convent. As she was pregnant, we referred to her as the Mother Superior! Our Maria was Emma Masand, daughter of our new head of infants. The part of the captain was played by a visitor from Australia, Danny Glasby.

Finale of *Anne of Green Gables* with some girls up in the house

Raj David and School Orchestra

The two made the most of 'I must have done something good,' causing the Loreto girls to hide behind their programmes. My directing took in the whole hall with the bride making her entrance through the main doors and proceeding through the audience, who, later, were glad to share in singing 'Edelweiss', (printed on their programmes), before the family escape to freedom.

Rajashri singing 'one rose' in 'Summer Song'

The year 1981 had us on Prince Edward Island for *Anne of Green Gables*. The famous house had to be built in the middle of the stage, so the action could be seen upstairs as well as down. It is, of course, a well-known story. Ritu Puri was our red-headed Anne, and she neatly smashed her slate each evening! In 1982 I added music to *A Christmas Carol* play that I had seen in England. With Greig's tunes from *Song of Norway* and three songs written and composed by one of the students, Christopher Masand, we presented *Scrooge*. The miserly fellow is doomed to meet four ghosts who cause him to wake as a different person on Christmas morning. Ritu Raj Rai played the part brilliantly, all through. His awaking was cleverly followed on the piano by Raj David, our talented music teacher. In 1984 it was the music and story of Anton Dvorak that filled our hall with exquisite music in our MP entitled 'Summer Song'. The famous composer gathers tunes during his stay amongst fellow Czech folk settled in America. It ends with a rendering of his *New World Symphony*, a lovely story, even if inaccurate, it gives space for some good character acting and singing. Rajashri Basumatari enjoyed her singing, and so did everyone who heard her! Ashok Pokharel surprised himself with some moving songs as Abe . . . Shailesh Prakash sang not a note but made plenty of them, as he played the composer. Ruedeeporn Sirapanivong sang us the sad tale of 'Murphy's Pig'. Vandana Pavamani gets married and then concludes that 'Once a year is quite enough'!

I might agree with her in reference to MPs! At the end of each year the school sings its Going Home Day songs, all printed in their annual calendar. One, the 'Leavers Song', came from a previous MP, 'Salad Days'. 'Summer Song' put another in it, 'Just Around the Corner'.

TALENTED STUDENTS

These shows displayed the talent of certain students, who would appear in the MP year after year. The prime example of this was Firdaus Rahman. She was one of a group of girls who took part in all the MPs from 1982 onwards. From a small part in Scrooge, she changed character in Ruddigore; and again, as Eliza in *My Fair Lady*; in *Carousel* (Julie); and finally, in *Brigadoon* (Fiona). Besides having a strong voice, she had an eagerness to get her acting authentic. For example, when taken to meet a Scottish lady in Darjeeling, she listened carefully to the way she spoke. So, in Brigadoon, she pronounced 'little' as 'wee'! In *Carousel* her distress over the death of her husband rather overwhelmed the lovely song that followed, 'When you walk alone, hold your head up high:' (which became one of the Going Home Day Songs'). Her acting was best perhaps where the character changed, as Eliza does in *My Fair Lady*. When she first carefully said, 'The rain in Spain falls mainly on the plains,' her change is quite unforgettable! Good actors and singers create good support from others taking part. Maneesh tackles long solos in *My Fair Lady*,

Carousel and *Brigadoon*; Arati Sharma falls sweetly in love in *Carousel*; and Ashok Pokharel as Colonel Pickering (in *My Fair Lady*) demonstrates his skill of 'playing the audience'. In my photo book, he comments, 'You were the person who made me realize that I could sing also, besides acting as well.'

Wide-eyed Juniors watch the dress-rehearsal

MPs
1974-77

FiDDLER
on the
RooF

Five daughters

Amal's visitors arrive
1975

Siamese Children meet their teacher
1976

The Finale of The Gondoliers   1977

MPs
1980-85

The
SOUND OF MUSIC

"Family Von Trap"
Sing at the Final
Concert

ANNE OF GREEN GABLES
1981

RUDDIGORE 1985

Three-legged Race at the picnic

1982
Reformed 'Scrooge' takes a well-deserved bow

Reformed characters
singing the "matter-matter"
song
With portraits behind them
that came to Life!

The Bridegroom also
designed four covers for programmes

Summer Song 1984

MURPHYS PIG

...sing a cast of **71**

MPs 1986-8

MY FAIR LADY
1986

Eliza dressed
for the
Ascot Races

Carousel
1987

"When I marry Mr Snow"

Brigadoon
1988
Meg sings
to the
kilted men

ELOCUTION

The English-medium schools in Darjeeling naturally stressed the importance of elocution – the speaking of English, as a language, clearly and correctly. MHS held internal House elocution contests, and then Interschool Contests between four local schools, with outside judges, sometimes from the British

Revd John Johnson

Counsel in Calcutta. I found myself involved in the training of students for Elocution. Choosing the best writers was very important. I introduced two sisters to the writings of Joyce Grenfell. Ratna Singh did 'the nursery school' when a visitor meets the class. It has that reoccurring phrase, 'George, don't do that!' Ratna did it in rehearsal at morning assembly. I had told her to look at the entrance doors whenever she corrected 'George'. I had forgotten that our senior master, George Fernandez, usually sat just inside those doors. You can imagine the reaction of the assembled school every time she turned and spoke to that naughty boy in her class! Her sister, Sunaina, did 'the school reunion' as 'Lumpy Latimer' who is 'wearing a woolly vest'. Again, I told her to look to the left when she said, 'Isn't that the girl who used to sleep-walk in our dormitory?' Who decided to move his chair to that very spot? Our principal, the Revd Johnston!

HOBBIES

Most of my hobbies had been started long before our work in India. I began sketching in my school days when encouraged by my Uncle Ron, editor of the *Weston Mercury*, who illustrated his 'Mendip Lore' articles with praiseworthy sketches of Somerset villages. From this developed my blackboard pictures seemingly enjoyed by pupils

Stamps for talks in church and schools

and staff. I painted some of the scenery for the MPs and ventured into oils with a picture of my dear Mum to take home for Dad. Woollen Rug Making developed during our courting days, and was continued in India., with a big mat of the DHR and other scenes. Stamp Collecting grew with my interest in geography, and was useful in its teaching and in children's talks in church. I sold stamps on my sale day stall each year at MHS. Reading continues to be a lasting hobby, and I have Nevil Shute, Libby Purves, Eddie Askew, and Jean Auel among my favourite authors. Many of my books support my work in Local Preaching.

WORSHIP

Every morning the school would assemble for Chapel, as you

Christian symbols on a stitched rug – made ten times!

might expect in a Christian School. We had our own hymnbook, compiled by Patricia Murray and the Revd Bill Jones. It contained many of their favourite hymns which I didn't know, but grew to love over the years. Scripture was read and a prayer made, usually by a member of staff. On Sundays, the Senior and Junior Schools worshipped separately. Mr Murray preferred the Senior Chapel should be held in the evening, before dinner. Revd Johnston had the Juniors before the Seniors both in the morning. I became much involved with the junior choir, who practised on a Friday evening after their meal, and in their sleepwear! On Sunday, of course, they were in their Sunday uniforms. (the boys with smart handkerchiefs in their top pockets!) I was invited to lead the Sunday service quite early in my stay at MHS. It was a new experience for me, but I drew on years of listening to other people, to learn how a service is constructed and a sermon to be written. There were experienced preachers already among the

'Do You Love Me?'

staff, and sometimes missionary preachers, parents of their children in the school, would give me new ideas. I recall how Karen Smith's father used songs of the show she was in (*Fiddler on the Roof*) to illustrate his sermon. He used 'If I Were a Rich Man' and 'Do You Love Me?' with the soloists actually singing them. I, later, used this idea myself, choosing to preach on a song from each MP – after it had been performed, and when everyone knew it.

CANDIDATE FOR MINISTRY

In the early '80s, I turned my future thinking to offering myself for Ministry in the Methodist Church, of which I had become a

member in 1978. My home minister the Revd Roy Shimmin told
me that I should first study to be accepted as a local preacher. This
I began in 1983, at first at home, and then back in Darjeeling. There
were four approved books in this preparation, with an examination
in each after six months of study. I passed all four within two years. I
also had to submit my own service experiences for approval. In 1984
I led services on twenty occasions, and preached in eight of them.

Stephen and Barbara's wedding

In one I used a song from the MP for that year 'The Fellow with
the Rose'. I became a local preacher in January 1985, at a memorable
service in the Chapel at Banwell. I returned to India for another
two years during which my application for training for ministry
was processed. In 1987 I reached the final weekend of interviews,
but I was not accepted. I immediately returned to my chosen work
in India, which was to finish at the end of 1988.

But in rushing back, I made one of the biggest mistakes in my life. I missed the wedding of Stephen and Barbara in Bristol. Judy was planning to go, and Bindu was to be a bridesmaid for the first time in her life. I knew that her dress had been made in Darjeeling. We were just about scraping together enough money for one and half air fares to the great event in England. David was already working at the Savoy Hotel, London. The great day was 20 June and photographs show a gathering of family and friends at the church and at the reception at the rear of their first home. I felt so very lonely that day, which has never been forgotten.

TTC

It was an honour to be involved in the Teachers Training College at Mount Hermon. I lectured in the methods of Geographical teaching, and also tackled some of their problems with Speech. I wrote a number of short playlets for them to speak in groups, also, I had them learning all sorts of tongue twisters, and began most sessions with writing *3333* on the

David's enrolment into the Salvation Army at the Rink

board, asking each to tell me clearly, what that number was. Many of them had the usual problem in pronouncing the *th* in English. The college was also expected to enter play competitions held in Darjeeling between various colleges each year. They practised on the school stage and would give a dress rehearsal to our students. They received much praise in the actual competitions in town, too.

It was around this time that we had an encouraging letter from David who was working in London. He had, at first, quarters in the famous Savoy Hotel, itself. Then, it was decided to move the men to a hostel some distance from the hotel. So, David had to use a bus to get to work. This took him along Regent Street past the Salvation Army Rink Church. A notice spoke of a Lt. Colonel Bennett speaking at the next meeting, probably the father of a SA boy David had known at Hebron School. He went there the next Sunday; found it was different man, but he so much enjoyed the full day of worship, eating, and general activities, that he was writing to ask us if we minded him joining the SA. We were delighted, and shouted 'Hallelujah!' It was at the Rink that David was taught to play brass instruments.

Army police at morning drill

TROUBLE IN THE HILLS

There were serious developments in Darjeeling and its district during the last three years of our time in India. The Gorkha (Nepali speaking) people were determined to create their own self-governing State: Gorkhaland. The area was part of West Bengal, which at that time had a Communist government based in Calcutta. So, most of their officials and employees in the Darjeeling district spoke Bengali. So, in some ways there was conflict between the two languages. Hundreds lost their lives, and thousands their homes. We were most aware of this struggle by the occurrence of strikes, often sudden and unexpected. Judy was more aware of these than I was. She did a lot of travelling, taking Tim and Bindu to or from Hebron School in the south of India. Their students from Bangladesh travelled home via Calcutta, and their 'party' could include our two. Booking seats on the trains was often difficult. There could be a strike in Siliguri and not in Darjeeling. Convoys of military vehicles would be created to take passengers safely in either direction. A brigade of army police was stationed on our playing field, using the gymnasium as their quarters. John Johnston did his best to keep the school open, with students working in the study hall when classes were forbidden, or allowing them to rehearse for the current MP. I think *Brigadoon* was the best rehearsed show we had ever done. All this tension and disorder made us decide to make 1988 our last year there. It was also considered that we should do so by our family at home.

An Ode to M.H.S.

They come from all around the world
To study at Mount Hermon:
Black and white, yellow and brown,
The high, the low, the common.

They run along your corridors,
Scratch names into your walls,
Laugh loudly in the quadrangle,
Pray quietly in the halls.

You teach them all the skills you know
With pen and ball and bat.
There is silence in the study rooms
And chaos on the flats.

You know each individual:
Their laughter and their tears;
You know what makes them happy;
You know their silent fears.

You see them in each phase of growth:
Their happiness, their strife.
You see them hesitate, then step
From youth to adult life.

All too soon the happy years
Will fade into the past.
But the love and knowledge gained
Remain until the last.

And each one leaves you sadly
For the goal that is in mind.
And each one takes fond memories
Of the life they leave behind.

Doctors, scholars, teachers,
Accountants, tradesmen, clerks:
In every single walk of life
Each one will leave their mark.

Each will find his niche in life
And remember you with pride.
The wisdom you imparted
Is carried far and wide.

And so for each and everyone
The wheels of life must turn.
All Glory, Alma Mater—
"Not for school, but Life we learn."

—Cedric DuCroix—
for my wife, Lynda (nee Martin)
EX-HERMONITE: AUSTRALIA

Chapter Nine
A Change of Direction

YATTON

We were home, at last, from India. This was to be in the village where Mum and Dad had lived for many years. He joined her in the Summer of 1988, and I had met up with John, soon after the funeral, to buy from him, his half of the house left to us by Dad. We were able to do this because we, both, had also inherited the home of my godmother, Alice – half each. Someone was looking after us!

41 Chescombe Road, Yatton

Tim and Bindu enjoy a first visit to Alderney

Alderney Chapel

Bindu had come home with us, but was to return to Hebron School to complete the school year there. I was unemployed for the time before Easter, and then obtained a term's work at Merrywood Girls' School in Bristol.

FROM TEA TO SEA

Then, on 20 April, we saw an advertisement in the *Methodist Recorder* for the need of a local preacher to be a lay pastoral assistant on the island of Alderney, in the Channel Islands. We had visited the larger islands on our honeymoon, but knew nothing about the smaller ones. I wrote to the superintendent of the Methodist Church in Guernsey to learn more about the job, and to apply for an interview. It was he whom I was to 'assist' by being the pastor of the little church on Alderney. Judy and I were invited to fly over to the island on 10 June. Air Sarnia flew small aircraft from Bournemouth Airport. Another couple for the interview flew with us, and when we landed, his wife said, 'Thank goodness that's over!' (We had thoroughly enjoyed it.)

Our interview passed most successfully. The people were very interested in our work in India, and in the fact that we had an adopted daughter from that land. I said that she was still at school there, but would be home within two weeks. We would like her to see her new home before a final decision. They agreed! We stayed the weekend, attending the Communion service on the Sunday morning. The church was a fairly old building, the third since the early days of Methodism. The people were very proud of the visit by John Wesley in 1797, seeking a harbour in a storm on the way to Guernsey. On 24 June Bindu came home, alone, so in the care of the aircrew, and I had to sign for my 'unaccompanied baggage' before telling her of a much smaller aircraft that was to take her to her new home. This time David and Tim came with us too. They liked the island very much; especially Bindu who was to make Alderney her home for many years to come.

PASTOR ON ALDERNEY

It was the islanders who gave me the title of pastor. They had had many before me. My predecessor, Norman Andrews, had been a caring, well-liked leader – a challenge for someone as untrained as I was. I had been a local preacher for seven years with experience of preaching restricted to the school scene, and services at home from December to February when in the UK on holiday. My first service was a Harvest Thanksgiving – which I had never taken before!

Some in my congregation were pleased to see that I had a university hood to wear for service. I was pleased to use my gift from Mum, and thought of her when I put it on. (Her dream for me was just a little fulfilled!) The chapel was a good place in which to speak – no pillars to obstruct the words spoken or sung. My training of youngsters in elocution ensured that most people could hear me. I wrote my sermons in long-hand: good blackboard script! But then I had to

Greetings leaflet produced for visitors in 1990

a warm welcome to
alderney

'He has made his light shine upon us' Psalm. 118.27

Let them give glory unto the Lord and declare his praise in the islands. Isaiah 42.12

Talk to the Christians who live on the island of Alderney and they will tell you that there is something special about this part of God's Kingdom. Although there are particular buildings set aside for the worship of God, as can be seen from the map, we do find that he can be experienced in so many places around the island – it's the quiet that hits you when you walk away from the airport...that firmness of the land as you step ashore...in the soaring notes of the skylark...in the purity of the seagull's plumage...in the restful pace of a walk through the streets...or along the cliffs...in the friendliness met in shop, inn and church. In all of these places we hope that you will find the true presence of God, give him the glory and, maybe, wish to declare his praise with those of us who live in these islands.

There is a strong ecumenical fellowship between the Alderney churches.

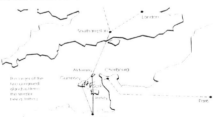

God knows!

by Pastor Geoff
Blackmore,
Alderney

THE expression 'God knows!' is often on the lips of people who are facing a problem in their daily living. Strangely, those who do not believe in God usually stress the first word, and those who do, stress the second.

It is the difference between those for whom the problem has no answer and those who believe in a God Who knows all about the situations that are faced and Who can be found within them.

So often, what seems unanswerable and disastrous to us is used by God to forward His purposes for His loved ones.

But what of the people who say 'I know', those who assure you that they know what you want, or how you feel, or what you should do?

I remember going into a tailor's shop in Darjeeling, India, and the owner showed me to a seat, saying: 'I know exactly what you want, sahib.' He didn't.

The Christian sympathiser should be careful in the use of this assurance.

We meet a woman on a bus. She has a heavy cold and tired feet and a bulging shopping basket – and it's pouring with rain.

'I know how you feel,' we say, but do we really? Do we know of the crushing news she received that morning, or the anxiety she has concerning a sick child?

We cannot possibly know all these things, but God knows. It's His love and concern that we must seek to share with those in need.

'Make me a channel,' we sing. But let it be an empty channel, with nothing of our own 'knowledge' to block the outpouring of God's grace to those whom He seeks to save.

A little sand upon the rails

by Pastor
G. D. O. Blackmore

IT IS nothing unusual to see trains in India covered with people, both inside and out. A seat on the roof is both cooler and cheaper!

There are, however, engines on a particular mountain railway – the Darjeeling Himalayan Railway – where there are two special seats on the front of the engine. Between them is a large metal sand-box, and the men who sit there direct a little sprinkle of sand onto the rails just in front of the wheels.

On the steep gradient it is possible for the wheels to slip and slide on the smoothly polished rails. The sand provides a little roughness on which the wheels can grip and so progress up or down the mountainside.

Closer home, how cool it is to be wearing sandals on these hot summer days! But there comes the moment when sand or loose stones get in under the toes and you hobble along, hoping they will be squeezed out within a few strides. If not, you will have to stop, unfasten the sandal and rid your foot of the irritation.

So a little sand can be both useful and a hindrance. Things can happen in our daily living that can make us stumble along the path

Thought for the Week

of life. We have to stop and rid ourselves of that discordant happening – a wrong attitude, an inability to forgive someone, a destructive relationship, a sinful habit.

Sometimes, however, the roughness in our lives will not go away, so we must use it to get a firmer grip on the track of life. There are many fine people who are fine not because they have had a smooth, easy life, but because they have faced the roughness of life

and made something strong, powerful and useful of it.

You may know that the oyster cannot produce a pearl without some irritant grain of sand which has gained access through a wound.

In Revelation 21, the Heavenly City is described as having 12 gates, each made of pearl. So it seems that entrance to that place is through the suffering which causes pearls to be formed in the lives of those who believe.

Jesus Himself showed us how His way of suffering has enabled all to find the gate to that Kingdom.

THOUGHT FOR THE WEEK

The Cross that opens the door

by Pastor
Geoff Blackmore

I HAVE recently taken several journeys from Alderney – flying to Southampton in one of our 'yellow birds' – and then travelling by train to and across London.

The railway ticket issued was valid for use on the London Underground. I just had to show the ticket to be allowed to proceed to an Underground train.

However, on one journey this failed. My tickets were from Birmingham to Euston, and then from Waterloo to Southampton. The London Transport official took a quick look at my tickets when I presented them to him in the crowded concourse and refused to allow me through his gate until I had bought an Underground ticket.

Puzzled by this, on my return to Alderney I asked our Rail agent how the official had known that my ticket was not valid for the Underground.

Pointing to a small cross he had made on another ticket, he explained that without that cross I would

not be allowed through the gate.

And that set me thinking! There was another cross placed on a hill outside Jerusalem many hundreds of years ago, and when men and women can see that cross acknowledged on their ticket for life's journey, then they, too, can know that gates will be opened for them.

Without the cross on my ticket I had to purchase for myself another to enable me to continue my journey back to Alderney.

But the ticket with a cross on it would have cost me nothing extra. All that was necessary for the Rail agent to know my need of getting to the other side of London at the time of booking.

Similarly, we too have to acknowledge our need of the Saviour's Cross on which His life was sacrificed freely for us.

"Thoughts"
in the
Guernsey
Press

UK 23
OVERSEAS 34

Christmas Newsletter
on sale in the
Church Bookshop!

GREETINGS

FROM...

Peace on
Earth

alderney

Steps to climb to Church

learn to deliver them, I listened to other speakers. Judy and I attended the Salvation Army in the evenings and I listened to the two young officers there. Also, tapes of sermons were sent to me from Yatton, and they were helpful, too. Also, I listened to what people complained about. The organist complained that everyone began to leave the church before he had finished his final rendering. I guessed that no one would move before I did, so I paused a couple of minutes before descending, with a 'Thank you, Graham' as I passed. I found, too, that people liked me to stand at the door when they entered the vestibule –after climbing the steep steps to do so. Another thing I learned in my new job, was to open my mouth for one lady who needed to lip read what I was saying; to announce the hymn numbers twice; and to allow a little time for elderly people to turn the pages. I was surprised, but very pleased, to be authorized to administer Holy Communion. Another part of my work involved the planning and leading of funerals. This took me into people's homes to learn something about the deceased person. Often this was not someone I had known, like the young man whose ashes were to be scattered out at sea. I was grateful for the boatman's advice, 'Check the wind direction, first, sir!' The crematorium was in Guernsey! So, if that was to be used, we would have to go to the airport where a Trislander, with some seats removed (to make room for the coffin), would take us (at its usual speed) down to Guernsey for further transport to the Crem. On my first visit there, I was surprised, after I had finished the service, to be handed an envelope

with the words 'your fee Pastor'. I didn't
know I was paid extra for a funeral! (£25 in
1990.) I had just one wedding, of an elderly
couple, both widowed. I had a number of
requests for marriage by divorced people,
but in those days the Methodist Church
didn't marry divorcees. (I think that is
no longer true.)

The wedding

One aspect of my work on Alderney
was the warm, Christian cooperation
between the churches. Every month
the leaders – Anglican, Roman Catholic, Methodist, Salvation
Army, and Friends (Quakers) would meet, usually at the vicarage,
for the planning and sharing in Christian Witness on the island.
There was an Ecumenical Bible Study group led by Catholic ladies
which Judy and I joined. Also, I was one of the leaders at a Service
for Healing held weekly in the big parish church. Judy enjoyed
singing with the Home League Singers at the SA. I found myself
involved in funerals at the big Church of St Anne, which would
be packed (everyone always went!); Good Friday Processions of
Witness, with a cross being carried through the cobbled streets
of the town; the annual Blessing of the Fishing Fleet, down at the
Harbour. In Lent we had meetings in each of the places of worship.
There were special services at the beginning of Alderney Week in
August, and on Twinning occasions with a town on the Cherbourg
Peninsula (France), I once had the task of reading in English my
four paragraphs of sermon, spaced, so that the vicar could give a
French rendering of what I had said!

We had many visitors to our church, especially in the summer
season. Several times, companies of girl guides would stay in our hall
beneath the church. We had camp beds for their use, a kitchen and

all essential facilities. They usually attended and took part in our Sunday Service. Although Alderney has its own States (Council), it is part of the Bailiwick of Guernsey. I, too, was on the Methodist Plan for the same area. Consequently, twice every quarter I found myself flying down to Guernsey to take services morning and evening in two of the nineteen churches on the larger island. It seems a lot of churches, but, originally, there were two circuits, one of which used the French Patois. In one church on the West coast, I still had to make room for one hymn in French, according to their choice! I needed two sermons, but I was advised to make one of them new. Bad weather on the Sunday morning could prevent flights, and I would want the new one for my own congregation! If all was well, a Guernsey-based preacher would fly up to Alderney, hopefully to return the same day. Because I took an evening service, I had to stay the night, and fly home on Monday morning. I did this on twenty-five Sundays during my four years as pastor, besides other flights to Circuit meetings. I also preached once on Sark, and made three visits to preach on Jersey, after that island undertook the expense of maintaining the pastoral work on Alderney and Sark.

I managed to boost my lowly salary with gardening on my rest day, and later teaching Latin at the Island's Prep School. Judy had a few private nursing jobs which helped. She tried to update her midwifery training on a course in Bristol, but was unable to complete this. However, it gave her a chance to live with Tim when he was settling to the world of work. Back on the island, how was my pastoral work developing, 'beyond the walls' of the church?

Although I had brought our car on the ship from Torquay, I decided that the pastor should walk whenever possible. My morning walk to the church took me through the town of St Anne. I felt it was good to be seen; and to speak with those I met, and to learn names. Strangely, the car was to help me in this, for on our first visit to one of the beaches, I lost the keys to the car. I had no others, so the car had to stay parked above the beach for about four weeks.

I could see it there from the air on my first appointment in Guernsey! Everyone got to know about this, and many would greet me with the phrase, 'Have you found your keys yet?' My son, David was able to get and send me replacement keys. The previous owner could remember its number. The car, by the way, had to be given a new number, as all cars on Alderney start with AY. I chose to add the number 288.

Sea for a trip

Regular visits around the island filled my weekdays: to speak at School Assemblies; take a service at the Jubilee Home for Elderly people – with taped piano tunes for hymn singing; to see patients in the Mignot Memorial Hospital; Sometimes, to make a regular visit to an elderly member of our congregation. Mrs Coe enjoyed rides to the coast where she would sit in the car looking out to sea. If it looked stormy, I would advise her that 'it looks a bit rough today for a trip out to sea.' She would chuckle, because she had told me, that she was to be 'buried at sea'! I might then take her to the Island Hall to change her library books, always heavy, large print ones.

Books – reminds me that I had a bookshop at the church. There was no other source of religious material on the island. I opened it at most happenings within the church. Some items were in large print. Several people ordered New Testaments and bible reading notes that were easier to read. I was supplied by Christian bookshops in Guernsey and Jersey. I introduced two books for general use within

the church. These were Good News Bibles in all the pews, and the recently published *Hymns and Psalms*. Later, we also had *Mission Praise*. We had a well-balanced choir of eight singers, two of each voice, led by Doug Truckle. He and his wife, Mary, were loyal friends from the very first drive around the island at the time of our interviews. I was able to arrange visits by a good evangelical choir from Guernsey.

School photo of Bindu

Finding accommodation for them was not always easy, especially for two nights. The well-known, blind singer, Marilyn Baker, made two visits. She was willing to sing to any size group –even visiting infirm people in their own homes, to sing one or more of her lovely, spiritual songs.

During my stay on this island, I wrote an account of the coming of Methodism to Alderney. It was an interesting project which took me in my studies to Newfoundland, for it was there that Jersey's fishermen first made contact with Methodist teaching; then spread it to Guernsey and then to Alderney. Many of the problems experienced through the early years were to some degree still to be found on the island today. Its isolation is one. And it is that that has kept Alderney unaffected by the pandemic during 2020! Then there is alcohol abuse. There are fourteen public houses on the island. I am not a drinker, beyond tea! As a pastor this was perfectly accepted, and possibly admired, but it created an invisible barrier within the community I was trying to serve.

Corporal in the Militia

Alderney is a peculiar place, with a peculiar mix of very independently-minded people. But it was a wonderfully challenging place in which to work, and the Kingdom does grow within the Islands, and extends to very many aspects of life there and beyond their beautiful shores.

(Quoted from my 'Advent of Methodism in Alderney' which helped me to win the Alfred Lamb Memorial Prize in 1994.)

JUDY CONTINUES THE STORY

We loved living on Alderney. I did lot of swimming in the cold sea. Geoff would drive me' ready to swim' to Arch Bay at the far end of the island, just three miles away. Sometimes, I swam to a neighbouring bay and back, then, quickly into a large towel for the drive for home. We loved to walk as well, breathing an abundance of really fresh air; pausing to pick huge blackberries in season; watching the evening sun sinking towards America. Geoff loved to sketch the scenery.

Although her class actually had only nine members, Bindu had plenty of friends. She would walk to school twice a day, coming home for her lunch. If they had been cooking at school, she would bring it home with her. Geoff had a special grace to say then! She gained some O-level passes which enabled her to enter college in Guernsey for a years' Caring course. Accommodation was found for her at the home of David and Gwen Moore, who are still interested to know of Bindu's adventures. She was, then, assisted with a Grant from Guernsey to attend Eastleigh College, near Southampton. So was Tim, when he went to Surrey University, at Guildford. The Channel Islands supported their youngsters extremely well for their Education.

John and Jenny Lewis – friends for life

Again, Bindu was to be a bridesmaid at the Luton Temple of the Salvation Army. Both David and Dawn were Salvationists and they were married on 23 May 1992. It was a pretty wedding, with sixteen members of our family present. The pastor from Alderney had a prayer to read. The couple had already bought a house in Luton, where they were to spend the whole of their married life of ten years' duration.

Visits from our family members usually happened once! The Trislanders only carried sixteen passengers. My mum and dad came twice. Friends from Indian days came, too. That reminds me, that our sea luggage from Darjeeling arrived, by sea, of course! We had sold much of our belongings before leaving so the boxes were few.

Within, our first year in Alderney, I made contact with John and Jenny Lewis. They had come to the island to establish a private Home for Elderly People. They had purchased the Royal Connaught Hotel, quite close to the Manse in which we were living. They became members of our church, and when the Home was eventually opened both Bindu and I found employment there. Clients were very few, never more than seven, and it closed some eighteen months before we left in 1993. They had found work with the Shaftesbury Housing Association which had large schemes of sheltered homes across England. After visiting them, Geoff applied for the appointment of deputy warden at Shaftesbury Court in Northchurch, near Berkhamsted.

Chapter Ten
My Final Career

SHELTERED HOMES

In the seven months of my being employed by Shaftesbury HA,
I learned much about resident, elderly people and those who care
for them. Our home was a two-bedroomed bungalow within a row
of similar homes. As deputy, I did a lot of cleaning of community
rooms and the sweeping of leaves on the paths joining the buildings.
It was autumn! Essential was a daily visit to each home to check on
the well-being of the occupants and to test their means of calling
for help. I enjoyed the work, and I think the residents enjoyed me.
The wardens were George and Carol West, keen members of the
local Baptist Church. George had a good bass voice and he invited
me to join his male voice choir. (I think I got the job because I
claimed to be a tenor!) Often, I had to sing my line alone, which
is seldom easy. We did several concerts, including one in our own
home. As a local preacher I also contacted the All Saints Methodist
Church, which was closely linked with the Anglican Church
in Berkhamsted. We joined a fellowship group there and I was
invited to take services in that circuit. I went to churches at Tring
and Ley Hill. The local Methodist minister was very supportive. I
was planned to lead at All Saints on the morning of 27 February
1994. Before leaving home, I received the sad news that my dear
brother, John, had died. He had recently begun a well-deserved
retirement from his work in Bath. He had a heart attack at home

Bindu working at the Connaught

John at camp

during the night. The ambulance crew were unable to revive him, perhaps they were not as well equipped as paramedics are today. His funeral was held in Zion Methodist Church in whose Scout Group he had always been involved. The church was full of Scouts of all ages. I was allowed to read scripture. Much of his later Scout work had been involved with the Woodhouse Camp Site, north of Bristol. A tree and a seat there commemorate his life. The seat bears the woodcraft symbol meaning, 'Gone Home.'

MALVERN

In March 1994, we returned from Berkhamsted to our home in Yatton, Again, I was looking for work. Judy's mum sent me a page from the *Malvern Gazette*. There was a teaching post she thought might interest me. It was not in my subject, but, on the reverse side of the page, was one from the local council wanting a 'warden for sheltered homes. Previous applicants need not apply.' I did, and ventured up to Malvern to be interviewed in a home close to where Mum and Dad were living. My experience with Shaftesbury interested them, and I was successful in getting the job that was to last me for the rest of my working life.

But first there was another wedding to attend. Bindu, for the third time, was bridesmaid to Caroline as she married Tim. They

Tim and Caroline's wedding reception

had met when Tim was doing a year's work experience whilst at Surrey University. This put him at the Christian Aid HQ in London. Caroline was nursing at the Central Middlesex Hospital, and they met at the Emmanuel Evangelical Church where many were from the Chinese community. After a traditional tea ceremony in the morning, their marriage was celebrated in St Paul's Church (Portman Square) before a crowded congregation, with wonderful singing and atmosphere. The reception was held within the same building

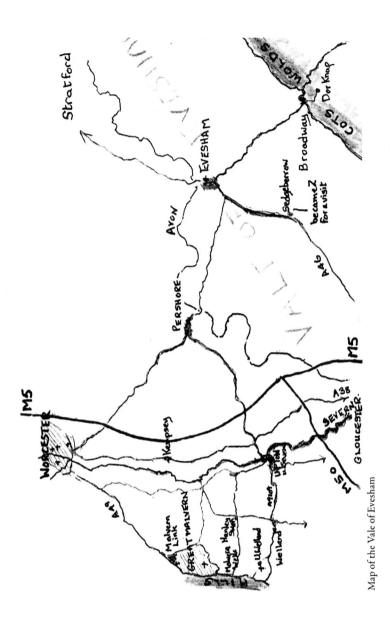

Map of the Vale of Evesham

as the church, beneath a banner proclaiming that 'We love because He first loved us'. They flew off for their honeymoon in Alderney!

My initial task was to act as warden of thirty homes in Malvern Link, housing over fifty elderly people. Our new home was a spacious upstairs flat with wide views in two directions, one towards the Malvern Hills and the other along the embanked railway, snaking its way towards Worcester. I began my daily work by stepping out of

Jamaica Crescent living room

our front door and knocking on that of our neighbour's opposite. There were eight within our block. The rest were all bungalows, in Jamaica Crescent, Lechmere Crescent and a mile away at Isobel Harrison Gardens. I had to visit each home every day. If they were fine, or absent, they might leave a sign, a note that could be returned through the letterbox, or a small stone on one side of the doorstep to be moved to the other end to show that I had called. If I was uncertain, I might look through windows, note undrawn curtains, or ask a neighbour if they had seen the resident. I had a master key which

I could use. Only once, in my seven and a half years, as warden, did I do so and find the person had died. Each home had a help line that I could use in such an emergency. I had, regularly, to test this appliance in all homes, and, always to encourage the people to use them. They had a pull cord in every room. Once I had a mobile phone, if they had a maintenance problem, I would contact the office, within their hearing, describe the problem, and get a time when help would reach them.

Warden leaving home

At Isobel Harrison Gardens, there was a community room where a weekly coffee morning was held. The residents and their friends would gather there. Once or twice a year they would go on an outing into the neighbouring counties and share a cooked lunch. All this had to be prearranged, by the warden, of course. Other residents could be picked up from Jamaica Crescent.

Wednesday was my day-off. Judy and I began exploring places reachable from Malvern. The town happens to lie at the junction of four Ordnance Survey maps. The first place we visited, was Ashleworth. On our return, I suggested that the next week we should visit a place that began with *B* and on a different map! By the time I had finished my work, we had gone through the alphabet three times! For some places, the 'sound' of the letter counted, e.g. *ex* for *x*, or *s* for *z*!

Over the years, the areas that I had to visit changed. They could be in any part covered by the Malvern Hills District Council. It might be other parts of Malvern, or in a village some way nearer to Worcester, or over the Severn to Kempsey. I became well known in these places, and I used my car regularly. Always, there was some new experience or problem to record, in some detail, on the Notebook pages to be filled in day by day. I used to enjoy doing that, and I was sorry that, as I retired from the work, it was declared unsuitable to record in such detail.

My other work, as a local preacher, also expanded during these years. I have note of sixty-four occasions when I was planned in the Malvern and Ledbury circuit. We were members of the Lansdowne Crescent Methodist Church and we also both sang in the Christian Witness Choir which practised and performed in their beautiful church. I also undertook the leadership of a House Group. The Imperial Group was named because it met in a large house in Imperial Road. We didn't pretend we were superior to any other group. Judy tells me that I remained the leader of this group for twenty-three years! Many of the members are indeed in a more heavenly place, now.

Chapter Eleven
Exploring the World

The Little Oxford Dictionary, that I often use, defines a holiday as 'a break from work especially for recreation, usually spent away from home.' The word itself reminds me that there is something 'holy' about this activity – that, in some way, God is involved in what happens. Our first day of married life was a Sunday, and we joyfully worshipped at the local Methodist Church. Holidays so often helped to 'recreate' our lives – in the places we chose to visit; from the company of friends who travelled with us, or invited us to their homes. Sometimes we met and made new friends.

Holidays involved us in travel, so the various means of travel were important. My earliest travel would have been by train to a south Devon seaside town. Then my dad became the proud possessor of a new car. Being the smallest, I often found myself sitting on a stool between my mother's feet (No seat belts in those days!) When the Scouts went camping, we sat in a furniture van with the doors wide open and all our gear around us. Our view, of course, was backwards! We sang for much of the journey. That was the sort of holiday that we made for ourselves, and that kind of holiday was repeated later in life. Even on a ready-made holiday, we enjoyed most what we did on the coach driver's day off! Train and bus passes were often very useful on days like that.

Some of the 'holidays' did occur as part of my work. As a geography teacher I might be engaged in 'field work'. Churchill

School was very supportive of trips away from school, even on the official school days. Staff ladies and gentlemen often took a leading role in these. There were annual visits to a fell-walking centre in the Lake District. In the spring term there were Holiday Fellowships for both girls and boys. Judy and I were involved in one to Towyn on the Welsh coast. It was our first holiday since our honeymoon, and we enjoyed particularly the steam railway there. Looking back, I remember that our first 'train-mad' son was born nine months later! Once I had passed my driving test, I had a vehicle of my own to use on many 'family' holidays. Some of these were shared with friends and their children. We went to Port Isaac with David and Margaret Holt; with John and Joyce three times to West Wales, on one of which my parents joined us; with Valerie and Clive Theobald northwards to Whitby. Judy had happy memories of younger holidays in Scotland: so, 1966 found us touring the Borders and then the Port Appin area, using caravans for accommodation. Newly-born David does not remember that holiday!

In 1973 I took a flight for my first overseas venture to Canada. David Holt planned to visit friends who had stayed in their Guest House. He invited me to share this carefully planned holiday through the weeks of August. We had discounted fares with Air Canada if we had four destinations on our tickets.

So, our flights took us to Toronto; to Calgary, with then a drive through the Rocky Mountains to Vancouver; a flight to Victoria (Vancouver Island), back to Vancouver and home. As geography teachers we were keen to visit as many 'useful' places as possible, e.g. A ranch on the prairies, a wheat elevator (pictured); a timber mill; or a Vancouver Salmon Cannery. Our day in Victoria was spent on bicycles! The whole experience was, also, of value as my plans for a new teaching place were developing.

During our fifteen years working in India, holidays were

largely taken in winter, involving
journeys to our 'homes' in the UK.
Judy made the journey five times,
and I managed twice that number.
Each February I would promise to
see my Dad again 'later that year'.
On my letters to him, I would have
a 'countdown figure' of the weeks
to go! We had two seaside holidays
incorporated within our journey
to or from the UK, at a Christian
Holiday Centre at Hua Hin, one
hundred miles south of Bangkok,
Thailand. We all loved the white,
sandy beach and the sea for daily
swimming or bathing, but watching
out for the sea urchins! Bangkok,
also, was a rich experience. When
our children were found a school
in the South of India, journeys were
made to the Nilgiri Hills. We usually
found Christian accommodation,
like Queenshill at Kotagiri, run by
our Hermonite friends, Joyce and
Duncan Wainwright. As far as was
possible, we travelled by train in
India. Reservations for a particular
train were to be secured months
ahead of the date of travel. Some
could be made in Darjeeling, itself.
Others, including air tickets, might

Wheat delivered to an elevator

Swimming at Hua Hin

Bindu with Grandpa

be secured by the Baptist Mission House in Calcutta. We tried to use British Airways, or Biman, the Bangladeshi Airways. The latter were cheaper and involved an overnight stop in Dhaka. Later, as aircraft increased in size, there were non-stop flights between UK and the subcontinent. Most of our flights were uneventful; problems were few and timing generally good. Only once was I diverted. When travelling to London, I was taken first to Hong Kong, then back to Bombay and on to Heathrow. Our children coped reasonably well travelling by plane or train. Tim's ears troubled him at take offs and landing. Bindu, also, cried then, when I took her alone to England for a memorable stay with Grandpa.

Our years in India opened our eyes to a wide horizon of places to visit, and of people to meet again. The 'Hermonites' are people who have been educated at MHS or worked there. So, many of our holidays since 1988, were centred on the homes of work colleagues or students we had taught or helped. It was good to be entertained by their friendship and to share memories of experiences with them. Some of these ventures were as a result of our children's outreach to distant places. Our visit to Malaysia was due to Tim's marriage to Caroline, daughter of a Chinese family there. Bindu's KG sweetheart sought her from Kathmandu, resulting in several holidays in Nepal in order to stay with them and their two wonderful children.

A number of MH staff had homes in Australasia. Others later made new homes there, like Stephen and Joan Lewis and their family. Bindu was to spend some weeks with them after Dipti, their daughter, had been ill. Judy and I were delighted to be invited to attend Dipti's wedding in 2002 in Melbourne. From there we went on to New Zealand staying there with Ian and Joy Reid (who joined MHS with us), and Graeme and Patricia Murray. The holiday ended with a two week visit to Papua New Guinea where a school colleague from Churchill School was working with the Wycliffe

Translators. The journey home from Brisbane, Australia was remembered by the bomb scare which sent our BA aircraft seeking the nearest airport, which happened to be New Delhi! David was following our adventure on line! He was able to meet us at Heathrow.

That visit to Papua New Guinea put to rest any interest of renewed work in the Mission field. We visited Ukarumpa, a huge centre devoted to the translation of the Scriptures into the languages of the people of PNG. It was the home of Joe and

Dipti and Bindu in Melbourne

Heather Patrick (nee Goodman). They ensured that both of us saw the activities undertaken in the Centre, especially for the education of the children of the missionaries, and in the Health facilities provided. All these were very well staffed. The Schools, junior and senior, were run as schools in the USA or Australia. There was drama, too. I watched a senior class acting out, in costume, the *Canterbury Tales*! There, too, we sensed fear in the air. The junior school was to be moved inside the safety fences evident around the whole community. After a wonderful stay there we came away with much to remember, and consider. Maybe the bomb scare on the flight home, might have strengthened a desire for the safety in our own home and countryside, sheltered by the Malvern Hills.

We made three holidays westwards to Canada initially staying with Rina and Roy Parry in Markham, Toronto. Rina shared midwifery training with Judy in Bristol. She was a great letter writer, too. On one occasion we took a coach tour from their home visiting places

Family enjoying icecreams at Green Gables, Prince Edward Island

in Ontario and Quebec. Then the next time, we headed West to use the Rocky Mountaineer train to reach Vancouver, and then on to Victoria. Yes, I was taking my wife to places I had visited without her! The last trip to Canada, in 2004, was planned by our son David. He hired a car at Halifax, Nova Scotia. and then drove us from place to place heading, primarily for Prince Edward Island. Our longest stay was on the island where we watched a performance of the musical, *Anne of Green Gables*, one of my MPs from Darjeeling days. The show was so wonderfully familiar, and was the apex of our holiday. However, we were then to visit places in New Brunswick and finally in Halifax where the Titanic Memorial Garden made an impressive conclusion to our tour.

We have had one holiday in the USA in 2013 to attend a School Re-union of Hermonites living there. David met and drove us long distances within a two-week visit. The actual Re-union was held in Las Vegas. There, they tried to take a photo of us seated at a gambling machine, to which we turned our backs! It was good to

meet with the small number who
attended the Reunion. Memorable,
too, was a two-night visit to the
Grand Canyon, with snow on its
fringes. It was January, after all!

MASTERSUN HOLIDAYS

A number of our holidays were
organized by a Christian Travel
Company named Mastersun. The
first in 1999 was a Cruise to the Bible
Lands of the Eastern Mediterranean,
starting from Crete; then to Israel; to

Cruise Passengers to Biblelands
(Mastersun)

Cyprus; to Western Turkey (Ephesus); Patmos; and finally, Athens.
Each place was studied *en route* with learned people to guide us.
The Christian fellowship was friendly and supportive – not too
fast or rapid. We worshipped in each place, sometimes singing even
where we were not supposed to do so! Once I was stopped and told
to cover my knees, as shorts were disapproved of. Jerusalem was
unforgettable, especially the Garden Tomb, proclaiming 'He is not
here, for He has risen'. There the guides were Christian; elsewhere
not always. Other Mastersun holidays took us Cyprus, Corfu and
Oberramagau for the famous Passion Play (once every ten years)
in 2000. We stayed in the home of a lady who had a small part in
the play. Never had we watched a play with 4,600 people totally
engrossed in what they were seeing. I was impressed at the number
of children who took part, even at the crucifixion itself.

EUROPE HERE WE COME

There were three holidays in Austria, besides two to Slovenia
which was reached from Saltzburg. There was one which followed

Audience before Passion Play stage at Oberramagau

Chalets near Aldelboden

Judy's favourite film, *The Sound of Music* She first visited Switzerland as a teenager and she was keen to share with me the town of Adelboden, and the huge chalets still occupied by visiting young people. Our first visit together was entirely by train in 1999. We made our first journey through the Channel Tunnel, coming through Paris to Basle and on to Chur for a week, and then to Brig enjoying, particularly, the wonderful Swiss Rail system, using our travel passes. Holidays like these were usually followed up by producing albums of photographs, sketches, and details of what happened and the people we met. Our shelves groan with their weight! Our most recent visit there was based in Kandersteg which holds an international centre for Scouting – now with girls, too! The Guide Movement has a camping centre at Adelboden, too.

It was Norway that I wanted to share with Judy. We went to the Fiord area in 1998, rather late in the season, with places already closed for the autumn. Toilets were far spaced, too, on that holiday! We visited Scandinavia in the year of our Golden Wedding Anniversary. The Saga Trip, led by an excellent lady guide (What a difference that makes to any holiday!) flew us to Stockholm; then an overnight cruise to Helsinki in Finland; then a flight up to Lapland; from there a cruise in a Hurtigruten ship all down the coast of Norway to Bergen, and a flight home. For many reasons, that was the best holiday (so far!). There have been other European holidays, taking us to Iceland for the geysers; Holland for the Spring bulb fields; Belgium to sing: France – for Paris and Annecy; finally, Italy for Venice and the lakes and mountains. We had one Rhine Cruise-a sunny week so hot without air conditioning, but still remembered every time the cuckoo-clock is working! Our home has many souvenirs, usually without names on them. The many angels on display started with one bought in Iceland; the staircase is lined with photos, often with Judy pictured. (I am usually the photographer)

Tibetan carvings are to be seen, as are crewel curtains from Nepal, but made at home by my clever wife. Flowery brackets in corners around the house are copies I made of such seen in Nova Scotia. Rugmaking, another hobby of mine, decorates with pictures of trains, mountains and Christian Signs. I have made ten of the last for various friends. (All the Tibetan rugs displayed Buddhist signs!) There are oil paintings, too.' on wall and screen. as the Japanese gentlemen might sing!

Judy feeds reindeer watched by tour guide

Chapter Twelve
Retirement

HANLEY SWAN

My retirement years found us in a cottage in the village of Hanley Swan, six miles from Malvern. It was part of an old house, but newly built inside! A visitor was to call it a 'dolls house'. It had four similar front windows and one central door. All the interior woodwork was new-unpainted. We decided to keep it like that. We wall-papered it throughout. The only long pieces were in the stairway! Toilets both up and down stairs, were a must, as old age loomed ahead. There was a long garden with room for two cars parking beyond it. We bought a Summer house for the garden, eventually to be full of tools. The cottage was very secluded. Visitors needed guiding; or meeting at the end of a short, private driveway. We bought Springvale Cottage from Colin and Roma Smith, who lived next door in Springvale House. When they felt age creeping on, they eventually built a bungalow at the bottom of their beautiful garden! They were the best of neighbours. Mine was the best garden I had ever had. Retirement gave me the time to tend it, and to actually see things grow, even if it took years.

Cottage garden at Springvale, Hanley Swan

Colin and Roma Smith with their newly built home

We once joined with other local gardens for an Open Gardens Weekend. On the first day, a birds' nest with eggs, was discovered within a honeysuckle bush just inside of the gate. By the Sunday,

UCC leader Sue brandishing office keys

My UCC card

they were hatched! The children, who tiptoed past it, were filled with wonder! The village had two shops: the village stores and post office, and the butcher. I made a ten minutes' walk to get my *i* newspaper, pausing to open it by the village pond, and chatting to people. In 2003, after our visit to PNG, we turned to settling into the community in which we were living. The first of importance was the involvement in the little Methodist Church in Upper Welland, a village four miles from Hanley Swan. There was a need for a new steward of the church, so I agreed to take up that position.

I had worked with stewards in the Channel Islands, and met those of other churches in our circuit through my local preaching. Through the many years that followed, Judy and I, with our friend, Heather Newborough, promoted coffee mornings, Light Bite Lunches, concerts, and other means of interesting the church goers. The church building was just long enough for carpet bowling, with the chairs pushed aside!

Back in Hanley Swan, Judy and I became members of a Handbell team –my wife with the highest; myself down with the lowest bells! We met in the home of Sue Spackman, opposite the butcher, from whom we bought duck's eggs as we had done in India. The bells? Well on our best days we were pretty good! It was always good fun! I drove countless trips for Upton Community Care in the sixteen years we lived in the village. Many of my driving customers lived there. I was one of the nearest drivers to them. Fares depended on the mileage driven, never on the length of time used. Most of my passengers were elderly, so my time as a warden proved very useful. I also took a monthly service in the Albion Lodge Residential Home for some years of that time.

With only two bedrooms (one my study) visitors overnight were rare. Roger and Margaret Billings came twice to enjoy the music on offer at the famous Three Choir Festivals, centred at one of the local cathedrals. A regular visitor was our dear friend, Christine Bennett, who tried to come down once every year, from her beloved Yorkshire. She was, sadly, separated from George, my mate of RAF days. We enjoyed her company enormously, and made return visits 'up North'! It was at this time I asked to join the Malvern Singers, a Mixed Group of some local renown. We were led by Edwina Ward with husband, Ron, on the piano. I enjoyed singing bass really for the first time. Local preaching was a continuing challenge, too. During the early years I was taking between twelve and fifteen services each year. The churches varied in size and distance: some were Anglican when there was a pulpit exchange. I was always given a warm welcome.

BINDU RETURNS

By the time it came to retirement, we had six grandchildren. Stephen and Barbara gave us Charlotte (born in 1993), Ella (1995) and Alex (2000). Tim and Caroline also gave us three: Daniel (1996), Grace (1999) and Lydia (2001).

All Three boys have done well in their respective professions. Stephen is a freelance oracle developer, David is a computer systems administrator for a global company and Tim is an accountant.

We had seen Bindu frequently whilst I was working in Malvern. With family cheap fares for flights, we went to Alderney where she lived in various locations. In 2007 it gradually seemed likely that her time on the island would end, especially after her MH 'sweetheart' Rajan Shrestha, had phoned us from Nepal the previous Christmastime asking to speak with her. I gave him her number in Alderney, and, as they say, 'the rest is history'. So, Bindu came home, with her cat! By May, she was on her way to Kathmandu. She returned in June saying that Rajan was asking his parents for permission to marry her. This was granted in August. Bindu received the news whilst holidaying with us on Orkney. At that time, Bindu was enjoying walking to her work at the Chase Care Home in Upper Welland, four miles each way. We insisted that an engagement party should be held in England so that all our relatives could have the opportunity of meeting Bindu's intended. This happened in March 2008. Instead of presents, a collection was made in aid of a

Left, Bindu and Rajan – engaged.
Below, wedding reception – family all
in red.
Bottom, following the band in
Kathmandu!

school and orphanage in Pokhara, Nepal. They had to be married at 10.25 am on 23 November, as decreed by an astrologer. So, we had to organise a holiday to include that great event.

David, Tim, Catherine and Paul accompanied us in setting off for Kathmandu. Before the wedding, we flew to Darjeeling. I explained to the assembled School why we were there, with a mention of a loving couple in KG! The weather was perfect. The mountains looked so near. Then, back over the border, to Nepal for the spectacular wedding on the twenty-third held at the hotel where we were staying. (It was Bindu's 'Home'.) After a huge lunch, we followed the hired band, by car and on foot to Rajan's home where his mother welcomed us. Two days later, a reception was held in a bigger hotel for a thousand well-wishing people. We wore red, the appropriate colour for a wedding in Nepal. We concluded our holiday with a trip to Pokhara, and a visit to the School there. Catherine, later, produced a splendid, colourful account of the holiday, which, in part, inspired the writing of the book you are now reading.

RETURN VISIT

The next part of this story has to be the appearance in our lives of two more grandchildren. Aasha was born in February 2010 and, within a month, we were in New Delhi to meet her. She was born in India, a fact, I believe, that eased the gaining of a British Passport for her. (Bindu has one having been adopted in the UK.)

In Delhi, we stayed at the home of Firdaus, last viewed in *Brigadoon*! We met several other Hermonites during our week's visit. Her driver took us daily to see the new baby. The next purpose of our holiday was to visit MHS, and there to direct a repeat of the MP *Anne of Green Gables*. We intended to spend sixteen weeks at the school. George Fernandez was now principal, and he and his wife, Saroj, had done much to lift the school from the disasters of the Nineties. We stayed in a house called Sunfower. The trees had grown so dense around it that the Spring sunshine had difficulty penetrating them to warm the house. It was extremely cold inside and we had to learn to cope with this. We did have gas on which to cook, which was a new experience. We used hot water bottles right

through to 4 June, the day we left. The house, too, was situated at the top of a flight of ninety-five steps down to the school drive, leaving a short walk to the main building. Judy had a somewhat easier climb to the Infirmary, but she found little welcome in

Sita receives her gift

the place where she had done so much previously. Young men, who brought us vegetables from the Kitchen were more pleased to see her. They, both, had been babies she had delivered into the world, years before. They were pleased to tell her of their own families!

Prior to our visit to India, we had been given the task of finding a 'film star'. Sita Chettri was a lady to be seen in a recent showing of films called *Indian Hill Railway* on TV. The first was based on the DHR. The Film was primarily about the people who

Judy meets Milan – one of her babies!

Newspapers report disturbed town

lived alongside the railway, not the trains themselves. Sita was a baggage coollie at Darjeeling Station. Her story was concerned with helping her eldest son to obtain admission to a college near MHS. A family in England had seen this film and wish to give a donation to Sita. They had sent us £50 to present to her. We had a photo made from a frame in the film, and on showing this to Eddie Tamang, then working in the maintenance department, he knew her immediately and was thrilled to drive us to the station to meet her and her son who had been enrolled at college. His English was good, which helped us! We handed her an envelope with the bank notes inside now changed into more rupees than she could earn in a year.

Within the school I was finding the directing of the MP very difficult. Girls were keen to take part, but boys were hard to find. I was to lose one through illness and another because he was expelled! (In the old days he might have been thoroughly caned, but that is no longer allowed.) Then the political scene in the district erupted into violence. One leader was assassinated, and reoccurring Strikes were to hinder any chance of the play proceeding. Anne was only to appear once-myself in costume with the staff on Freak Day when they dress as students prior to the annual sale day. I managed to lead the worship on three Sundays, and, then, to preach at St Paul's School of which an exTTC teacher was rector. John and Nina West also attended the service and we all had lunch there.

We had two welcome escapes from our cold home. One was to accompany a girls' netball team to Dr Grahams' Homes at Kalimpong. There we were warmer-and cleaner! for we had our first shower of the holiday. Our girls were disheartened by the robbery of their belongings the night before their matches

The would-be 'Anne' and the only Anne

with other schools. They performed poorly. Sport at MHS was far better organised than in years gone by. I found that my rehearsals frequently competed with various practices. There was, also, an atmosphere of fear in all parts of the building. So many doors were locked and the keys difficult to obtain. I only got on stage once in twelve weeks!

The other visit, deliberately organised for us by Hermonites, Ramesh and Kavita Lakhotia who own a big hotel in Gangtok. Having visited us in Sunflower, they soon had their vehicle at the foot of those steps to take us to Sikkim. We had a wonderful weekend there! On our return to Darjeeling, we discovered that another Strike was imminent. An escape from that gravely disturbed area was arranged to help us find safety in Nepal, at Pokhara. There, in the heat of June, we were able to see more of baby Aasha, but having also to dodge a falling ceiling fan! We were relieved, at the poolside, to receive news of rearranged flights organised by David in the UK. What did we learn from this venture? Perhaps for the first time, that we were now too old to do things that had been easier to do, during the many years of working there.

A GOLDEN EVENT

The year 2011 saw the celebration of Fifty Years of our marriage. We chose the National Trust Croome Park near Upton upon Severn for family and friends to meet with us, have lunch in the old NAFFI kitchen and Dining Room, walks around a very sunny Park, and finish with a strawberry and Cream tea, with a suitable cake to cut in the Croome Court.

Rajan and Bindu, with baby Aasha sixteen months old, were there, we smiled to recall that that was the age of Bindu when we first saw her! Our treat holiday that year was the splendid tour of Scandinavia, previously, described.

The years 2012–13 found me back at school! I joined an 'Open the Book' team of Christian adults who presented dramatised Bible stories to junior school children. The team operated at Northleigh School in Malvern. With a headteacher being a sincere Christian, we were made most welcome and encouraged to make weekly visits. It was wonderful to be speaking to 300 children waiting eagerly to hear the story. I was asked to narrate the stories which others led in costume with the inclusion of the children. Our leader, Mary Lawrence, was a governor of the school, so was able to go there to train some children for special parts. It thrilled me to realize that in reading the stories, I was losing any occurrence of stammering.

Open the Book logo

Indeed, I still feel that 'Open the Book' cured me! The stories were written in a language that children could understand easily. Reading them with all the experience of my career gave me immense satisfaction. The team was led with excellent preparation and prayer. Mary, and her husband Robert, lived a short walking distance from the school. After each performance, we would retreat to their home for coffee and preparation of the following week's story.

Increasing age makes one more aware of illnesses and mishaps. I was frequently poorly during my time in India. I had hepatitis twice, and in 1981 I had a partial thyroidectomy. My hearing was increasingly affected with tinnitus. By 1997 my diet was controlling my type-two diabetes. A fall on ice within a Swiss mountain left me with a weakness in the left arm. For each of these ailments, one copes by learning how to live with them or despite them. For example, I was to discover that automatic gear changing was a bliss of which I had not been aware. (when driving the left arm has little to do).

Judy, too, has had a fair number of health problems to contend with. I have tried to be fit enough to help her when necessary.

Bindu and Rajan's second child, Romeo Liam, was born in October 2013 at the modern International Hospital opposite their new home in Grande Towers, Kathmandu. He was under intensive care for the first ten days of his life. Soon, then, he was home attending to the business of growing into a fit, lively boy. He appears to be very intelligent and is wonderfully loved by his sister, Aasha. There was one way I could be of help to him. They were having problems getting Romeo a British Passport. (he was, of course, born in Nepal) Bindu phoned to ask if I could get the assistance of our MP in this process. Apparently, there are strings of influence an MP can pull. I had no idea of how to contact one's MP. I went to CAB (Citizens Advice Bureau)

Romeo with passport

Stephen and his hole cutting tool

and asked them. Their screen told them that our MP had a surgery that very afternoon in Malvern. Harriet Baldwin was very interested in my request for help, and she undertook to make it possible for our grandson to have his British passport.

At that time, too, we had the company of Stephen living the week with us whilst being employed in Worcester. This lasted for five months into 2014. He returned home each weekend, but found the time in the evenings to do a number of jobs for us. He kept us, too, in touch with the rest of his family, whom he often phoned. I remember how surprised he was at the lack of street lighting in Hanley Swan. I think that is still true!

REUNIONS

Mount Hermon School now has Hermonites living across the World. This results in there being a regular number of Reunions planned and organised in various countries. The best attended was probably that to celebrate the School's Centenary in 1995. This was based mainly at the School itself in Darjeeling. Ten days in November were filled with activities in and around the school and college, and included a weekend at Gangtok, Sikkim which was very special. Graeme Murray was pleased to open a new cricket ground there, by demonstrating some skilled batting! He was one of four principals who attended; the oldest being David Stewart.

We were able to visit our second Reunion in January 2012 held at Las Vegas. Only a dozen Hermonites and families attended, but it gave us the chance to see the area where David now lives. It was my first visit to the USA; the immigration officer said, glancing at my date of birth, 'What took you so long?!'

Five years later, in December 2017 it was the turn of the Hermonites in Nepal to organise a brilliant reunion in Kathmandu and Pokhara. We added to this another stay with Firdaus in Delhi and spoke at meetings with Hermonites there, who were not travelling up to Nepal. David accompanied us; we always feel well looked – after when he is with us. Tim joined us later in Kathmandu, and stayed longer to trek in the Himalayas. There was, of course, plenty of time for us to see Rajan, Bindu and their two children. David saw us safely home.

BERROW COURT

Judy glad she does not mow this lawn at Berrow Court!

Home was a new one. In July 2017 we moved six miles into Upton-upon-Severn, a name that is appropriate indeed, as the river expands its course as I write. It has never, I am told, flooded the forty-year-old buildings of the Court in which our retirement continues. It was planned to have a special reunion for this 125th Anniversary of MHS at the end of 2020, but the coronavirus has stopped all planning. Our Christmas newsletter described in some detail the family gathering we enjoyed at Christmas 2019. That was our most recent time of hugging Bindu and her family. We so enjoyed watching Aasha and Romeo enjoying their first pantomime! This year (2020), of cancelled and uncompleted holidays has, nevertheless, found us learning how to cope; how to live, as we face whatever each day brings.

Judy gives a final comment:

> Our sixty-five years together have been very happy ones.
> Not only because of the interesting lives we have led,
> The places where we have lived and worked; the holidays shared.
> But made all the better, because of the person that Geoff is.
> People have said of him that he is the kindest person they have known.
> Since his eightieth birthday, life has been very different for him.
> He was sad to give up driving for Upton Community Care at that age.
> He also misses his garden at the cottage; now we only have a small patio.
> But he has made that very colourful with many potted flowers.
> On various occasions when I have been ill or disabled,
> He has proved to be a competent and caring nurse and house husband.
> Thank you, Geoff.

Geoff has his say:

JUDY

It took me a long time to give her that first kiss,
But I did so, because, then, I was sure that I loved her.
It took me some time to write a long letter,
But there was always then another to answer.
It took us a long, separated time to train and to learn,
But, after five years, we proclaimed our love in marriage.
It took a long time to turn to overseas mission.
But it gave time to be congratulated on my three splendid sons!
It took Judy some time to find her calling fulfilled.
But the servants and children needed her care, lovingly provided.
We worked in Mount Hermon, where others could see us,
But she never saw me teach; or I her actual nursing!
Together we sought a daughter; Ruth must be somewhere here,
'May I speak?' and my request was granted.
And that sixteen-month darling was ours! Our family completed.
Judy has, since, been a wife to a pastor;
A support to a warden, and a passenger of a driver:
A knitter of pullovers and mower to a gardener; a listener to a preacher.
She speaks in questions: seldom demands.
She loves me with every dish she prepares;
She prays with me; sings with me; drinks her tea with me:
But, at the moment, we dare not kiss!

Our daily Quiet Time, reading a hymn, a Slice of Bread, (Scripture) and comment from Our Daily Bread, prayers from our own prayer book, where always is found a prayer by Eddie Askew, whose writing has greatly helped us; and finishing by remembering whoever sent us a greetings card. Every member of our family is prayed for by name. We end our prayers to God made in the name of Jesus, His Son. Sometimes, we might finish with the words of Joseph Hart's lovely hymn:

'Tis Jesus the first and the last,
Whose Spirit shall guide us safe home;
We'll praise him for all that is past,
And trust him for all that's to come.

Epilogue

Geoffrey David Owen Blackmore passed away on 9 October 2021 after a short illness.

This book is dedicated to his memory as it was one of his last wishes that this should be published. The proceeds from this book will be sent to the Darjeeling Railway Community Society who help local people who live along the railway line that became such a part of all our lives.

In the funeral tributes, one of the former students from Mount Hermon wrote these words:

> They say there is a reason
> They say time will heal
> Neither Time nor Reason
> Will change the way I feel
> Gone are the Days . . .
> But in my heart, You will always be there
> The gates of memories will never close . . .
> I miss you more than anybody knows . . .
> Love, Respect I send from here
> Always and forever
> Till we meet again . . .
>
> Rest in Peace my dearest uncle,
> friend, mentor and above all, my teacher.
>
> Arati Sharma (Bhatt)